# RELENTLESS REDEMPTION

No Pain, No Shame—Born to Reign

By

Laura-Lynn Tyler Thompson

Harrison House
Tulsa, OK

# CONTENTS

*Our history becomes His story!*

# A PRAYER FOR YOU

For all of you who have touched my life and for
those who honor me by reading this book,
I bless you with this prayer…

*I pray for divine connections, favor and ironic honor to take their astounding and rightful place in your life. I pray that the mistakes of your past become so distant that you wonder if they ever really happened, while the successes of your future become so awe inspirin g that it will be difficult to comprehend or believe that it's true. I pray for clarity, good judgment, wisdom, godly power, strength to endure, and an open heart to receive more than you could ever ask for or imagine. I pray that the God who saw you in the darkness of your weakness will raise you up in His supremacy to spacious places, larger lands, indomitable territories and unpredicted conquests.*

*May His outrageous plans lift your hope to new heights. May God increase your expectations to what He is truly capable of, as you experience the most unrelenting and overwhelming breeze of His unfailing, unconditional, and incomprehensible love. May you truly know that He sees you and is captured by your brilliance as you shine with magnificent beauty, not only before Him, but also before those whom you serve so graciously. May treacherous enemies and looming valleys be carried away as if they never existed. May truth lead you to justice and freedom. I pray that you will receive glimpses in small humanly-bearable portions, in shadowed moments, of how matchless His love is for you. For if we truly knew or could experience the whole of it, would we be able to stand?*

Laura-Lynn Tyler Thompson

# ACKNOWLEDGMENTS

I would like to thank my patient and wonderful children: Larissa, Aaron and Tyler for giving me room these last few months to finish this book. They asked with anticipation in their faces "Are you done?" Then they would realize by the look on my face that no, I was not done yet. They extended grace and kindness, while cheering me on. Thanks for bringing me tea a thousand times Larissa!

I would also like to thank my husband, JT, who sat quietly in the room, not disturbing me, just being near me while I wrote. I love you! Your smile and gentle words, "I miss you," encouraged me when the book consumed my days and nights, when the end seemed too far away to ever reach.

Thank you my dear friend, Jacki Poulin, who edited my book and spent countless hours reading, encouraging and giving me godly advice. You brought great comfort to my heart in ways that words can't express. This was not an easy story to tell. We will be friends for life.

Thank you Sandi Tetrault, for reading some parts of this book and texting me to keep me focused; you are a rare friend. I am so grateful for your prayers and love. I would also like to say a special thank you to my author, speaker friend, and sister in Christ, whom I have never met, but feel as though I have, Judy Reamer. Your advice on the content was pivotal and helped me get the balance right. (It's strange how God brought us together...too funny!) May your next book be blessed beyond measure, Judy.

Thank you Colleen, for taking care of so many little things so I could focus on getting this big thing done. You ignored Mr. Bundy and Stan so you could help me...what a treasure you are. I would also like to extend thanks to my Clothing Club Girls: Nancy, Rachel, Lorna P., Lorna W., Charmaine, Bev, Aaron, Bonnie, Laura, Vera, Deean and Barb. You all have laughed me through this chaos for almost 20 years!

Thanks to my awesome cousin Velma, for being there through the trauma. We have a lifetime of better days now. And finally, Lorraine Meller, thank you for picking up the phone because the Lord told you to call me and thank you for laying aside your entire agenda to help me do a final edit of this book. You are an incredible woman of God and He knew I needed you right now. You have blessed my soul!

Thank you to my publisher, Harrison House, for taking a chance on me. I love the spirit of your work. You have been the driving force and momentum behind my long days and nights of writing. God bless your work for the lives you will influence and powerfully change through the authors you embrace.

# FOREWORD

*And they [earnestly] remembered that God was their Rock, and the Most High God their Redeemer.*

- Psalm 78:35

I could not have written this book, overcome the despondency in my life, or had any success to enjoy life without God's Relentless Redemption. I did not know how He would get me out of the mess I had made for myself. I thought I was through——destroyed and disqualified. But God's mercy never let me go. His grace overwhelmed my soul.

God's relentless pursuit of a broken, discarded girl became a staggering story in my life. I was compelled to tell it all because I wanted my life to be a beacon of light to anyone out there who thinks they have failed too greatly to ever be used by God, or who have been lied to by the enemy of our souls and fed the blatant deception that God does not love them and has forgotten them.

One thing I have found to be true is that we have all been created with a magnificent destiny to fulfill. It is irrevocable——but it can be missed when we fail to realize that God has already set the plan in motion for us to have an incredible journey. He's already done something astounding.

Just in case you botched up your one and only life, He bought you a new one. If you yield to His power, He will breathe new life into you...even when you've failed, even when you've messed up beyond repair, and even when you believe there's no hope for the sorry state that you are in.

As long as we stay close to Jesus, no devil in hell is going to stop God's plan for our lives. I have become tenacious in my pursuit of all that God has for me. In light of the priceless life He's given me, I no longer have a choice. I am His and His alone. I've decided there is nothing that will block my path with Jesus. He taught me that my weakness is a gift because I must rely on Him to bring His great purpose to pass in my life. It never was and never will be about my righteousness; I have none.

We have redemption and it's astounding! We are bought back at a price too high for what our tarnished lives deserve. We need to dream again and dare to believe that "it ain't over until it's over." According to our faith, we must rise up and walk from our broken place.

**He took my HISTORY….I took His DESTINY!**

I've asked God if I could stop talking about all my failures and mistakes and just become the airbrushed person people see on a poster. Then everyone would assume, through my work on television, that I've lived a pretty good life. However, the gentle voice of the Holy Spirit let me know that my story of pain and shame is truly about what *Jesus* did, and not about *me* at all.

On this basis alone I am compelled to tell my story, as one who has been the beneficiary of a present so magnificent and undeserved that I could never have predicted the outcome. My story is the story of relentless redemption that never let me go, even when I was at my very worst. God has repeatedly required that I live my life with brutal honesty and transparency so He alone would get the glory. My failures, regrets, lost reputation, identity crisis, depression, seemingly insurmountable circumstances that encompassed my soul, and fall from grace that should have been the end of my destiny are the stories that God can use.

I have lived the dark nights of the soul and found the "Light" at the end. Jesus is the "Light." He is my Source, my only Hope, and my Anchor in every storm. His Truth has rendered every lie useless. I stand tall in Him; He is my Rock. All other ground is, as you know, *sinking sand*. Now I have no pain, no shame, and I know I was born to reign. It's a miracle—a Jesus miracle!

It's easy to read these words and gloss over the significance that is written here. But in the following pages, I will tell a story so astonishingly desolate, yet so full of God's mercy, I trust it will breathe hope into anyone who feels they have destroyed all prospect of walking out the true calling that God has ordained for their life.

Every one of us has a gift that we were born to give the world. When the enemy sees us begin to walk in our call, he sets a snare to rob us of what is rightfully ours. If you have become ensnared, you may think all is lost forever. Redemption means you get it back. More succinctly, Christ already bought back your destiny; you only need to receive it.

My story reveals a person with dreams, hopes, talents and hidden gifts, along with many liabilities, failures, mistakes and errors that should have meant the collapse of the destiny God intended for me. This book will help revolutionize the thinking of those who are shattered, disqualified, ineligible, suffering, or broken, who need to know that God has not rejected, forgotten or abandoned them. It will empower you to rise up and walk in your providential appointment.

God has outlined the path to freedom clearly in the Scriptures. It is so outstanding and simple that anyone could miss it. I stumbled through the darkness for years to find it, but you don't have to. The Word of God is quick, yes, quick and powerful to the pulling down of every stronghold in your life. *"For the Word that God speaks is alive and full of power [making it active, operative, energizing, and effective]; it is sharper than any two-edged sword, penetrating to the dividing line of the breath of life (soul) and [the immortal] spirit, and of joints and marrow [of the deepest parts of our nature], exposing and sifting and analyzing and judging the very thoughts and purposes of the heart"* (Hebrews 4:12).

My story is written for one reason alone—so you too will realize that you have an incredible destiny waiting for you, regardless of anything you think might have deemed you undeserving of it. An inconceivably blessed life is promised to those who are willing to accept that when they are weak and broken, it is the right time, even the perfect and necessary time, for their most stunning adventure to begin. For you see, it will never be by your own might or power that such a voyage will ensue. It comes only in the humble yielding to the One who has the ability to grant promotion, success, endorsement, achievement and triumph *in spite of you.*

When you begin to line up the thoughts and purposes of your heart with the Word of God, you will encounter such an emancipating touch of God's power that you will never be the same. I remain staggered at life's turn of events. God loved me in my weakness, held me in my brokenness, never left my side through failure, and set my feet in a spacious place to fulfill the destiny that was ordained from the beginning of time. And He did all of this in spite of ME!

Redemption is Jesus' story given to us. It is relentless, unstoppable, unconditional and irrefutable. It is the space between our failures and eternity. By His fathomless grace, I'm living in it. *And you can, too!*

# 1

# ROCK BOTTOM

*In all their affliction He was afflicted, and the Angel of His presence saved them; in His love and in His pity He redeemed them; and He lifted them up and carried them all the days of old.*

- Isaiah 63:9

I woke up with a jolt as the alarm clock went off a little too loudly for my liking. I felt through the darkness with my eyes shut to find the off button. *Are you kidding me,* I thought. *Is it that time already?* I routinely traveled from the West to East Coast to tape *The 700 Club Canada,* so I lost three hours of time per trip. This meant that I should have gone to bed three hours earlier than usual. But my internal clock kept saying, *Why am I trying to sleep right now? It's 8 p.m.* Then in the morning when my clock read 6 a.m., my internal clock would say, *It's 3 a.m.!!! Why am I up?*

It usually took me a couple days to adjust to the time change, but it only took about three minutes to realize that I would get up anytime, do anything I needed to do, and go anywhere I needed to go in order to live the life that God has granted me today. I am walking in outrageous, relentless redemption. My friends marvel, my enemies sneer, and my family still stands with their mouths agape. I have been given a journey that's supernatural, miraculous, and crazier than my mind could ever conceive. It rises above anything I had ever expected on my best day—and it has nothing to do with me. I did not create, manipulate, or design this journey.

As a little girl in Uganda who was born to missionary parents, I hoped that one day God would use my life for Him. But a tragic turn of events and my own destructive miscalculations along the way made me think I was disqualified forever. I thought I was done in, destroyed and finished for good.

As I was on my way to tape a show, I fast tracked through my regular morning routine. The excitement grew as I raced through the hotel lobby with my huge suitcase in tow, waving hello to the front desk attendant and signaling the first taxi in line to get me to the studio. After a quick coffee stop, I was on a mad dash to the start of a very long shoot day.

As we drove to the studio, I usually engaged the taxi driver in a chat about his life. On this particular day, my cabbie was devastated by a suicide pact made by his friend's daughter that had left four teen-agers dead that week. "I'm so sorry," I said, as I took my suitcase from the trunk. I paused and told him that God was the only hope for all of our families. He nodded and gave me a kind smile.

As I made my way to the professional powder room to begin two solid hours of hair and facial overhaul with my favorite make-up artist, Jolene, I wiped back a tear. What a desperately sad world. I prayed, *Jesus, help me to tell them who You are in such a way that they will know who they are in You. Give me the words. We are all so desperate without You, Jesus!*

Three hours later, looking a little more glamorous than the frightening face that greeted me in the mirror when I woke up, I was ready to start the day. We began by praying and asking God to do the impossible as we do the possible. Brian Warren, my co-host, then prayed one of those deep, powerful, awe inspiring prayers, invoking the name and blood of Jesus over every word that would be spoken. A quiet hush descended into that large, spacious studio and the warmth of the presence of the Holy Spirit engulfed our hearts. "Father, we pray that You would be the words we speak—nothing of ourselves. When we are weak, You are strong." I took a deep breath and we were ready to begin.

After we shot one episode, I paused quickly to take a call from home. I never knew what chaos would break out with the high-risk youth I cared for. Indeed, this call was very important. It was 14-year-old Jasmine and she was threatening to run away again because she claimed to have no freedom. It's true, she didn't have much freedom because she would head straight out to the streets into prostitution. She started prostituting when she was 12 years old and now it had become a way of life for her. Jasmine was one of the toughest kids we'd had in six years of working with troubled youth. She was mean, very strong, and vile to the core when she wanted to be. But I sure loved her!

Our senior producer, Todd Cantelon, called us to the set again and we began reading through the next script on the teleprompter. With the hustle of a long production shoot schedule, it's hard to find a second to breathe, let alone a moment to ponder the last 46 years, but that's exactly what I found myself doing on this particular day. We taped three shows and then I was able to take a break as my co-host

Brian - former two-time Grey Cup winning football player, now pastor to a nation - did a ministry teaching straight to the camera.

I stood against the back wall and surveyed the large beautiful scene before me. I had grown accustomed to being in television production with long days and too much fun for words. With a sigh I whispered under my breath, "How did I get here?" Speaking nationally about my precious Lord and Savior Jesus Christ every weekday of the year— how did this happen?

When I was six years old, my dad preached a sermon to our church in Uganda. With tears streaming down my face, I promised to devote my life to God and serve Him for all of eternity. Only Jesus knew the desperate place He pulled me from after my life had become messed up beyond recognition through my own choices. I shook my head slowly in disbelief; it could only be God.

During my 13-year television career, I've had the pleasure of meeting extraordinary people like Dog the Bounty Hunter and his wife, Beth. I've also interviewed movie star Josh Duhamel. I've chatted on red carpets with Jesse Metcalfe and 'the Fonz' Henry Winkler, as I physically shook to think my childhood crush was now a guest on the daily show I was doing.

Even more significant were the men and women of faith I met such as Tony Campolo, Josh McDowell, Pat Robertson, Dr. Gary Smalley, Patsy Clairmont, Gigi Graham, Thelma Wells, Liz Curtis Higgs, Bill Hybels and Dr. Gary Chapman, to name a few. They have all been an inspiration to my life.

I thought of my favorite passage in the Bible that sums up my existence. "For you see your calling, brethren, that not many wise according to the flesh, not many mighty, not many noble, are called. But God has chosen the foolish things of the world to put to shame the wise, and God has chosen the weak things of the world to put to shame the things which are mighty; and the base things of the world and the things which are despised, God has chosen, and the things which are not, to bring to nothing the things that are, that no flesh should glory in His presence. But of Him you are in Christ Jesus, who became for us wisdom from God—and righteousness and sanctification and redemption—that, as it is written, 'He who glories, let him glory in the Lord'" (I Corinthians 1:26-31 NKJV).

Had there been any more foolish, more weak, more base, or more despised person than me—if not in the eyes of others, then certainly in my own eyes? I had wounded God's providential will and purpose for my life so astoundingly that I thought I would never recover. Yet, here on this ordained day, I stood in this hidden corner of a studio with no pain or shame. I had been so emotionally bruised beyond recognition that only the work of a Master Potter could take this clay jar full of gaping holes and broken fragments and re-make it into a vessel of honor.

Even as a young teenager I had big dreams. I knew God's hand was on my life and I hoped that He would use me in a magnificent way. But the years proved to be far more hazardous than I expected. As I stood soundlessly in the studio, I knew it was not my hands, nor will-power or talent that brought me here. It was only His amazing grace that extended clemency and pardon to an undeserving girl—relentless redemption for the years that were stolen!

My mind wandered back to the previous decades when decisions were made that affected the rest of my life. I recalled the darkest moments when the consequences and weight of what I had done unleashed a landslide of horror and pain. In a flash, it was as if I were there again.

"I CAN'T DO IT! Jesus, I just can't do it," I sobbed. The rain poured harder than I had seen in months. I cranked up my windshield wipers, but nothing helped. Was it the rain or my tears that blurred my vision? I couldn't tell. My physical heart was in so much pain, I could barely breathe.

As I pulled over to the side of the road, I began to heave cries from a place I didn't know existed. I slumped over the steering wheel, cramping my pregnant stomach. *What have I done? God, what have I done? Make it better Jesus…I'm so sorry, I'm so sorry.* The gut wrenching sounds that came from my chest and out of my vocal chords surprised my own ears. The pain was unquenchable and the deed unchangeable. Some wounds are so deep that even a cleansing cry will not salve the trauma. There was no medication, remedy, answer, or prayer that seemed enough to heal the destructive laceration in my life.

I sobbed, "If you take this child, I will go back to my husband and …" I gripped the steering wheel as if it were a life preserver, "…and I will try again. Jesus, I don't know how to change what I've done. Please God don't leave me, I'm sorry, I'm sorry, I'm sorry…" I gasped and breathed, heaved and sobbed. Forty-five minutes passed and the tears still wouldn't stop; there was no relief from the hades of my soul. I had never known such sorrow or irrevocable agony.

I thought of how I could ask the church for forgiveness. Pastor Bob was certainly a man of God and would forgive me. Even though I had betrayed the congregation by leaving my husband, I could throw myself at their mercy and beg them to pardon my shame and disgrace. I could live with the humiliation, and in time, maybe I would find their love again. The man, whose child I now carried, had just an hour before spoken to me so harshly with such vile words, I could not believe my heart had betrayed me into believing I loved him.

But even if I could convince the church to allow me to grace the steps of their house of worship, I knew I could not convince my husband to take me back. I had already tried. I sincerely and humbly asked John to find it in his heart to pardon me for what I had done and to forgive the unforgivable. I begged him to consider that perhaps we could start from the bottom of this "hell hole" that I had created through my reckless actions and we could ask the Holy Spirit to fix me. I knew I was very broken and had no idea how all my pieces would ever be put back together again.

I'm not sure why I didn't realize that there was no true romance between John and me until I was literally walking down the wedding aisle. I had always longed to be married and have a Cinderella love story. Indeed, my wedding dress was staggeringly gorgeous, with beaded embroidery, satin bows, and tiny little buttons from the nape of my neck to the small of my back. The wedding included five brides-maids and groomsmen, little ring bearers, something old, something new, breath-taking bouquets, a garter belt, two hundred guests and dreams of living happily ever after.

I had waited my whole life to get married. When I was a little girl, I would play for hours in the front yard pretending to be the bride…and now that day had finally arrived. The very first inkling that something was amiss on that sunny wedding day so long ago was my initial glimpse of the groom who waited for me at the end of the long church aisle. I always thought I would feel different at that moment. I imagined having loving, excited, and passionate feelings for the incredible man I would spend the rest of my life with. But as I walked down the aisle with my arm linked through my dad's, I became uncomfortably conscious of an uneasy feeling in the pit of my stomach. The fact that years of dreaming and months of planning had brought me to this exact moment surely meant that this was the right thing to do, wasn't it?

John smiled broadly and seemed completely oblivious to the little firestorm that was beginning to brew in my being. His adoration was evident; he was a very good man. He was loyal, kind and gentle. *What is my problem?* I wondered. We had written our own vows and I had used the words spoken by Ruth to Naomi, "I will do you good and not harm all the days of your life."

As I finished giving my promises at the altar, I silently said to myself, *Well now I've said them; I have to keep them.* An ominous foreboding swept over me. I had always been a carefree, happy, quirky, funny girl, but the wedding video taken that day betrayed the truth, now captured forever. The camera doesn't lie. There was a very different woman standing there—a somber, grave, sad looking bride.

I planned the reception down to the smallest detail, but all I wanted to do was leave. Everyone stared happily at us and tinkled their glasses over and over again. Laughter rang throughout the evening and my mom and dad were so proud. The toasts were given; the groom responded and choked up in declaring his undying love for me. Why did I feel nothing but dread? We had remained true to our commitment of waiting for sex until marriage. I remembered how I had hurried the wedding date so I could finally experience the joy of sex. I looked hard at the man now enthralled to be marrying me. Who was he? *Why was I getting married?*

Later that night, the wedding party accompanied us to our honeymoon suite and they had one final toast to the 'amazing day' we had just experienced. They all respectfully and quickly said their goodbyes and gave us a final hug. I found myself saying, "You don't have to go so soon." My matron of honor just looked at me as if to say, *What is wrong with you? You've been waiting for this night your whole life!*

When it finally came time to consummate the union, I claimed fatigue. John was always the perfect gentleman so it was nothing for him to overlook his virgin bride's innocence and hesitancy. The next day we flew to L.A. and drove to Palm Springs for our honeymoon. The drive seemed to take forever. We were a good team; I told him where to go and he did it, making every exit and on-ramp that we were supposed to take.

This reminded me of how the last two years of courting had been. John was always so good about letting me have my way, my choice, my ideas and my decisions. *Why did that feel so dull?* I stared out the window and realized there was a big problem. I didn't want to talk to my new husband or kiss him, let alone do anything else.

We pulled up to a Kentucky Fried Chicken restaurant and I asked him to get me the usual two-piece chicken meal. I settled into a booth and looked out into the parking lot. In the reflection of the window, I could see John ordering our meal. I suddenly took a deep and unexpected breath. I swung my head around to look right at him in person. *Oh my Lord, who is that guy? I don't even know him. Seriously, who is he? Why did I marry him? What have I done?*

# 2
# BINDING DECISIONS

*But you shall [earnestly] remember that you were a slave in Egypt and the Lord your God redeemed you from there.*

- Deuteronomy 24:18

W ho can explain the willful silliness of a 21-year-old girl? Before my wedding, there were comments about me being "a bit young to get married" and probably what they meant was that I was kind of immature, even for a 21-year-old. There was no doubt that was true. I was a 'throw caution to the wind' kind of gal. That's why I dated my first serious boyfriend against my parent's wishes. He turned out to be a cheating maniac who went out with most of my friends behind my back.

The first time I found out he had cheated, my heart was broken. The betrayal, disloyalty, and sheer pain of being in love for the first time----whatever that actually means----and then finding out that person is simply a snake in the grass cause tremendous hurt. At 16, you can be that dumb. With all those crazy teenage hormones, you believe you have found Prince Charming. When that love turns out to be the most debilitating, emotionally damaging experience you have ever had, it's not cool. Nevertheless, my harsh judgments would one day come back to accuse me.

I had chosen to live life on my own terms, sometimes against my parents' and other authorities' wishes. I was headstrong and believed I could grab adventure by the tail and go for the ride of my life. No one could stop me, and why would they want to? I wasn't doing anything wrong that I could see. I had never been drunk or smoked cigarettes, and certainly not pot! I had also chosen to remain pure. I didn't dance, except if the Spirit led me to do the two-step in worship. I didn't chew gum in church and only snuck out to one movie in my life. I was nearly perfect. Well, except for cheating in school, for which I got the paddle and was *definitely* repentant and sorry for my despicable actions.

There was rebellion in my young heart during my high school years that God began to deal with me about. I didn't like to be told what to do and I questioned everything. It wasn't all bad to probe the legalistic rules that made no sense, except that when I didn't get the answer I wanted, I determined in my heart to do exactly as I pleased.

This began a pattern of upheaval and painful discipline that seemed to have to be administered over and over again. I would break and be repentant once caught in a misdeed, but I had an issue of character under-development that I was not willing to acknowledge. Life was not black and white to me so it really bothered me when people were rigid and legalistic. Ironically, I could certainly see the error in other peoples' ways. When our pastor of many years fell morally and was defrocked, I thought his punishment was fully deserved and had little compassion for him.

I had some good points about how the rules of our church were too rigid. Later on, there was admission by the church leadership of that time that the legalistic rigidity of the church overshadowed the true message of God's grace and His desire for truth in the inward parts more than outward performance. In spite of the war that waged within me against legality, God's presence touched me profoundly through my teenage years at camp and at the private Christian school I attended. Even so, my anger would burn when restrictions were imposed that did not come from Biblical commands, but were rather manmade ideas of righteousness.

So here I was a married woman, having chosen to do just as I pleased. I did not understand why I had gotten married. I did not know why I felt nothing for John and I was completely clueless as to what to do about it. I was numb. A dark cloud descended over my being and I felt as though I was stuck in sinking sand. I knew I could not escape the marital vows I had taken before God and man.

To his extreme credit, John did not complain. He was supportive and wanted to give me time to overcome my issues. I could not tell him I felt nothing towards him. How could I hurt him in that way? I simply told him that I didn't know what was wrong with me.

When we returned from our honeymoon in Palm Springs, I began a new job downtown. For months I rode the Skytrain with thousands of busy people. I watched them closely, especially the women, to see if they were happily married. I saw young girls practically making out with their boyfriends. I was envious of their passion. I had waited 21 years to have that kind of relationship and now that I was married, I felt dead inside.

I remember the long rides to work, staring out the window with an empty, passionless soul. I had no remedy for the detachment that separated the once joyous, hopeful, carefree girl from this shell of a person who now existed. Where had I gone? I was so lost and there was no way out. I thought about telling someone what John and I were going through but it was too embarrassing.

Maybe we could get an annulment since it had been impossible to consummate the marriage, but the thought of explaining my reason for requesting such a thing was daunting. Who would believe me, and even if they did believe me, they would think I was crazy. After all, what on earth was my problem? Was I not still morally responsible before God to stay true to my vows? God hates divorce and He would be so angry with me for leaving my marriage. I was trapped and the chains felt heavier and heavier.

Worse yet, my new job put me smack in the middle of a bunch of stock traders who were fast talking, women hungry males. This held little interest to me as they had the moral fortitude of mating rabbits. Even in the stupidity of the gross error I made, I knew these were not the kind of men I wanted. But there was one guy who was extremely polite and kind. He seemed to be different from the rest. I knew he held a temptation for me so I tried to avoid him, but his office was right beside mine and we would chat here and there. One day his friend called me over and said, "He thinks he is falling in love with you." My heart raced.

The friend asked if I would be willing to meet up with this guy that weekend at his place just to hang out. Inside my head, I yelled

*"YES!"* But I knew God had a call on my life, even though it was buried in a pit somewhere. It took every ounce of character and every bit of sheer willpower to open my mouth and whisper sheepishly "No, I can't do that." I don't know where I drew the strength to resist this temptation. I breathed silently, *God help me to stay away from him.*

A moment later my boss signaled me to follow her, "Can you come and see me in my office?" She scared me. She had big hair and beady eyes with massive amounts of eyeliner and mascara glopped on in chunks. She was not the friendly sort and I had only seen her laugh out loud once at work, then when she realized what she had done, she quickly wiped the smile from her face and returned to her serious "Certified Accountant" face.

As I followed her down the hallway, I put my personal drama aside and sat down in her office as she closed the door. This was not good; it was Friday. *People always get fired on Friday.* Instinctively, I put my feet flat on the floor, hoping it would brace me for whatever she had to say.

"This is not working out is it? I don't think you are enjoying this job and I don't think it's right for you," she said. I looked at her, wondering if it had been that obvious. It was true; I hated accounting with a passion. I had already, numerous times, wrongly put the debits in the credits column, and frankly, even after having my mistake explained to me several times, you might as well have described nuclear fusion.

It was an act of God's mercy that I was told to pack up my desk and not return. I took the bus home and burst into tears when I saw John. He was truly wonderful. "Who cares what they think, you're awesome and you will find the right job. It's ok, don't worry about a thing!" It was a warm comfort to have this good man embrace my pain and demonstrate such kindness.

As I recount the undeserved and particular blessings that were shown to me in those trying times, I am reminded of 2 Corinthians 12:9, "My grace (My favor and loving-kindness and mercy) is enough for you [sufficient against any danger and enables you to bear the trouble manfully]; for My strength and power are made perfect (fulfilled and completed) and show themselves most effective in [your] weakness. Therefore, I will all the more gladly glory in my weaknesses and infirmities, that the strength and power of Christ (the Messiah) may rest (yes, may pitch a tent over and dwell) upon me!"

To think that God, who knows the end from the beginning, knows everything we have done wrong and the mistakes we will make in the future, lines up little miracles for us all along the way to enable us to bear the trouble. What love! Even though God saw a storm cloud looming heavily over my journey, so great that it could potentially destroy my destiny, His favor and loving kindness pitched a tent and dwelt over my life.

What kind of amazing grace is that? It's the kind that's not dependent on performance; it's given to those who belong to Him. When the accuser comes, he has no right to speak against us. God will take care of His own, even when damaging, unchangeable decisions and mistakes are about to be made.

On Monday morning, I dropped over to my parents' place to use their Yellow Pages directory to find a new job, and by a sheer miracle, a call came to their house for me. I had been married and had not lived there for several months so it was a surprise that the woman asked for me by name. She was a job recruiter and had an opening at a firm downtown. She was going through old files to find the right candidate. "Um, are you just calling me out of the blue?" I asked, as I noted how odd it was that this call would come to my mom and dad's house. I marveled as I made an appointment with her.

I drove home with gratefulness for God's grace. He knew exactly what I needed and sent the answer before I even started searching for a new job. *Aren't You mad at me God? I am in such a mess of my own doing.* Though small, it was a significant sign that such a strange provision would fall into my lap, even though I felt as though I had made a tremendous error.

I got the job as a receptionist in a small, family owned real estate company. I loved going to work and started to really like those very wealthy, kind people. I was embraced and felt my work was appreciated. It was a safe place and it gave me some space to think. Although I was busy, I couldn't stop musing over my predicament with John. I turned the matter over and over in my brain, trying to figure out how I got here and how to get out.

It had been extremely physically painful to try to have intimacy in our marriage. One year of this turned into two, leading to three and four years with no answer in sight. Several sessions with a counselor revealed John's continued compassion towards me in my broken state. It was noted by our counselor on more than one occasion how blessed I was to have a man who was so patient and willing to love me in spite of this difficulty we shared. I had to agree.

I would look at John and feel grateful—but felt no chemistry, passion, or romance towards him. It wasn't his fault; he was a great looking, honorable, and decent man. As I looked for the counselor to give me answers that would fix my problem, I realized she had none. All I knew was that I was desperate for help.

We explored numerous possibilities and remedies for our situations but never came up with any real solutions to my crisis. None. The only possibility was death, "till death do us part…" I didn't want to die, but I barely wanted to live. Not like this. Maybe John would pass away unexpectedly and I would be free. I couldn't believe I would think such a terrible thing. I am embarrassed now to admit that I would often think of the relief I would feel if John would pass away so I would be released. But those thoughts only made me feel worse about myself.

I had lived for romance and wanted the fairy tale life. This was definitely not it! When the business of the day was done, I would go home on transit and once again stare aimlessly out the window. I felt imprisoned, hollow, and entombed in a dark dungeon I had created for myself. If all of life is a play, I had written a horror with no end in sight. I lay trapped in its undeterminable outcome. I knew this was totally my problem; it wasn't John's doing in any way.

The Christian church and the Bible did not seem to have any definitive antidote for my situation. I would ask God what to do but I could not hear the reply. There was no remedy for the disastrous vow I had made. Divorce was not an option. Did I want to be one of those terrible divorcees who were shunned and scorned? Of course not! I had been taught in church that "God hates divorce" and I truly perceived it meant that He hates divorced people. So, I would not dare to become one of those.

Sinking into a despondency that never left my conscious thought, I began thinking about having a baby. That could be a possible solution. It would give us something to love together. Although John and I struggled greatly, we found a way to make the biology work. It was one of the most amazing moments of my life to hear I was pregnant. I was awestruck that my body would carry a beautiful child and I would be a mom. It gave me so much to dream about again—so much to anticipate. I had not experienced this kind of joy for years. Maybe this would change everything.

In spite of my natural fear that my womb was about to grow to 1,000 times its regular capacity, I was ecstatic. The baby was only the size of a poppy seed when I found out I was pregnant, but I loved that kid! I watched faithfully as my tummy grew. I followed the progress and growth at each stage in the baby guide. I marveled that his little heart was beating by week five. The joy that flooded my soul was incredible and for the first time in a long time, I hoped some kind of miracle would happen between John and me. Indeed, it was an incredible season to watch our baby develop week by week. We both knew this would be amazing.

Months passed and I quit my job to be home with our new baby. Finally, labor pangs began. Forty-nine hours later after a grueling experience that left me feeling like I had been captured and tortured by a militant group of army thugs, Tyler was born. He was adorable, although he strangely resembled Yoda—bald and beautiful. I held him for a few minutes as he lay there with his eyes closed. At one point he opened them, looked at me, then shut them quickly and refused to open them again. I wondered if he had heard all the screaming.

I was initiated instantly into the world of sleep deprivation, extreme exhaustion and colic. The first night in the hospital, Tyler woke up every 45 minutes. The second night, the nurses noted the blood had drained from my face and offered to do the 3 and 5 a.m. feedings so I could get more sleep. In the morning, feeling guilty for having left him with the nurses, I went to see my brand new baby and the nurse looked at me and said, "Oh, you're *HIS* mom." I looked at her for a brief moment, puzzled, but had no idea why she had that certain tone.

After being home from the hospital for only 24 hours, I called and said we needed to return to the hospital immediately. The receptionist would not put me through to the maternity ward. She transferred me to the emergency department instead. I knew they would understand that something was terribly wrong. Tyler cried most of the night and would only sleep for 1½ hours at any given time.

The doctor listened patiently as I explained that Tyler was in pain and perhaps one of his gall bladders was stuck in his appendix. She suggested gripe water and noted that babies usually overcome colic by three months of age. *Colic*!! Gasping in exhaustion, I realized I was not going to get any help from these people.

Over the next few days I did my best. My mom stayed over one night to help, but I didn't sleep the entire evening because Tyler was up every 45 minutes crying. It was draining. One morning, I had fallen back to sleep on the couch when I woke with a jolt. I had been sleeping for over two hours. It was a miracle! I looked over at the baby bassinet and Tyler wasn't there. Panic gripped my heart. I looked on the love-seat under a throw, under the cushions… nothing. I ran to my room. *Oh my goodness, someone had stolen my child!*

I raced into Tyler's bedroom and relief swept over me as I saw him sleeping quiet as a mouse. Who on earth had put him in his crib? I had no memory of doing it. I shuffled back to the couch and flopped down just in time to hear the doorbell. A wonderful lady from church and her daughter were delivering a meal for us. She took one look at me and told me it would get easier very soon. How did she know I was struggling? Was it my puke stained pajamas, my disheveled hair, or the fact that I was inexplicably carrying a mop?

The crying went on for months, sometimes Tyler cried too. I developed a stomach ulcer from the stress. In the midst of this torturous season, in between his colic outbursts, there was this cute little smile and an occasional giggle. I fell in love with this little bundle of trouble, but somehow I knew he thought I was an alien who had captured him and was holding him against his will.

One day, I held Tyler in my arms and with my biggest smile I flapped my lips together and made a whizzing sound. He took one look at me and broke into a terrified shriek. I knew it was early morning and I looked hideous, but to actually see my precious boy burst into tears just because I made a funny face and a motor noise, saddened me. I didn't understand why he didn't seem to be bonded to me; I felt like a failure.

It was much more difficult to be a mom than I had ever imagined. I found myself once again sinking into a sad place. I didn't understand post-partum depression, but I was sure that having a baby was not the antidote to my previous sadness. I desperately wanted my relationship with John to be different. There was a settling into life with our handsome boy and a mutual love for his growing personality, but it did nothing to heal the deep chasm between us.

One outlet that brought me great joy was leading worship and a Bible study at our church. My pastors, Bob and Linda, were gracious to give me the opportunity to explore the gifts they saw in me. They were also true friends who tried to help John and I navigate through the difficult intimacy issues we faced in our marriage. We all believed God would heal our marriage and move us into the purpose He intended for us.

One friend later told me that they thought John and I were being groomed to eventually lead the church. I can only say that at the time, my mind held no such thoughts. I simply wanted to be used by God. I understood I had some rare concerns in my personal life, but I was grateful that God gave me opportunities to serve Him.

I was asked to speak at the ladies luncheon at church and I remember feeling at home while sharing from my heart. The presence of the Lord was with me and I felt a recurring sense that my destiny was tied to speaking and teaching the Word of God. I recalled how a good friend of mine who is now a pastor, Paul Maines, once said to me as a teenager that there was a powerful mantle of anointing on my life.

But he gave a strong caution to me saying that to whom much is given, much is required, so I needed to govern myself carefully.

Whenever I was called on for any of these cherished opportunities like leading a Bible study, I poured my heart and soul into doing the best I could. There was a powerful knowing in my spirit, despite the complications of my marriage to John, that God had predestined a plan for my life and I fully intended to embrace this vast journey that He was just beginning to unveil. I recalled the way God had touched my heart as a child in Uganda. Nothing could separate me from my first love, my Heavenly Father, my Savior—my only true source of joy.

During this time a snare was laid for my soul by the enemy, whose familiar spirits knew my life well. They knew my sorrow and my weakness. As I look back, my long-standing confusion with intimacy and the trapped feeling I had lived in for almost four years had begun to take its toll on my spirit. I found myself falling into a pit of loneliness, hopelessness and boredom.

A man from our church began to drop by because his girlfriend was attending a university nearby. While he waited for her night courses to finish, he would drop in for coffee. Zack was a sociable and fun individual. As these occasional visits continued, I began to look forward to our frivolous conversations, which led to the beginning of an obsession similar to drug addiction.

What started as an innocent friendship, a subtle escape from my sad reality, soon turned into a fatal attraction that had a shocking grip on my being. I began an affair that had no foundation in God, values, principles, or good judgment. I remember hearing someone speak on how affairs are more about your personal need to feel validated. An affair is your ego's quest to be adored, sought out, put on a pedestal and longed for.

As time marched on, I contemplated ending this terrible fascination with darkness. But when I tried to talk to Zack about it, he would just laugh at any attempts to end it. The war between good and evil left a voice in the depths of my being screaming at me daily, *Stop! Run away...run away now!*

After about two months, I was entrenched in a deception that I had not seen coming. One day I wrote a goodbye letter to end our relationship and gave it to Zack. Two hours later, I began to shake physically and literally went into a desperate state of panic. I knew I could not dump him. It only took a phone call to rescind my written wishes. The terror of that attempt left me even more immobilized.

Zack offered no help whatsoever to fend off the tsunami that was quickly approaching the shores of my life. I literally lost my mind. I became driven by my desires and relinquished all logic. I tried to think through what I was doing, but frankly the compulsive thought of when I would next see Zack or hear from him was all I could concentrate on. I became dependent on that connection with him every single day. It was like an electrical current going through my being. I could not discern that it was a monster that would eventually almost take my life.

I remembered a woman who had poured her heart out to me a few months earlier about the misery of her life and some difficult issues she had faced with disloyal and cruel men. We talked for awhile until John came to pick me up. She gazed at him with jealous eyes, "Wow, some people have it all!" She shook her head looking at me and I knew she envied what she thought I had with John. Indeed, I wished we had that amazing relationship that she thought we had. But the man with the cool clothes and handsome physique that she was looking at did not hold the key to my heart.

I sold my good judgment for a meal of selfish, indulgent gratification. Like a stupid woman, unable to see the devastation that lay in my path, I ventured forward going deeper and deeper into an abyss. I began to plan my escape from my marriage. I built a wall between wisdom and myself. One part of me knew this was wrong. Another part of me was relieved to find that I could experience intimacy with no pain.

I began to rationalize, to some degree, that my circumstances had forced me to do this. Every time I met with Zack, it fed the worst nature within me. I succumbed to its hold on me. His charisma swept me off my feet. I was so deceived that I believed he was the soul mate I was supposed to be with. I thought we had missed this love connection because I had married John too soon, in error. I simply rationalized every bit of wrong to try to make it right. When I felt too guilty, I tried to call it off several more times, but realized I was powerless to stop this soul addiction.

It's interesting how time and experience clarify feelings that you thought were one thing, when in fact, they were something completely different. I thought I was in love, but all the time, it was a terrible trick of the enemy sent to destroy me spiritually, emotionally, mentally, and eventually affect me physically. Satan is a liar and his tactics have not changed since the dawn of time. He hates us and he slithers his way into our psyches any way he can. He has one goal according to John 10:10, to steal, and to kill, and to destroy.

# 3
# NO GOING BACK

*O Lord, You have pleaded the causes of my soul [You have managed*
*my affairs and You have protected my person and my rights];*
*You have rescued and redeemed my life!*

- Lamentations 3:58

I remember the ominous moment when I walked downstairs in our townhome and felt a cold chill physically run through my veins. I stopped and looked around, a bit surprised because the house was warm, but the atmosphere was somehow frosty. I stood frozen in my tracks and wondered what the problem was. Dread gripped my heart as I realized for the first time in my whole life, *I could not muster, nor feel, any tangible sense of the presence of the Holy Spirit.* It is the closest I can imagine to what hell is like——the absolute absence of God.

I was familiar with the experience of Jesus' breath on my face and His hands holding mine. I had known this warmth since my earliest recollections. I gave a quick shiver as I embraced my own body to feel some heat. I knew in my heart that He could not commune with my spirit in this state. I realized how Jesus must have felt on the cross when He cried out, "My God, My God, why have you forsaken me?" upon realizing His Father's presence had left Him.

I slowly turned and shuffled to the kitchen. I had no clue how to turn back the clock on the decisions I had made. How would I regain the "first love" for my Savior I had known? It was now a precious pearl that I had lost in my state of confusion and resentment. I had no power to help myself; darkness overwhelmed my spirit.

My sleep began to be disrupted every night with guilt and anxiety. Paranoia was something I had not known until then. My carefree adventurous spirit had always been undergirded with the powerful knowledge that God was with me, even if life was not going the way I had hoped.

I continued to buy into the deception. I truly believed I had now found the love of my life and I could not live without him—come hell or high water. Although I had once cherished my love for God, I now could not stand the thought of being without Zack. He pursued me ceaselessly, playing into my ego and my desire to be wanted and adored. He wanted us to be together and he didn't seem to care that his or my reputation could be harmed.

I had shared with Zack the intimacy problems that John and I experienced and he wholeheartedly asserted that was proof that ours was a union that was never meant to be. He assured me I could probably have gotten an annulment and that I just needed to move on. I latched on to anything Zack said that would make me feel better about what was happening. However, I didn't feel any better; I felt shame and guilt.

I finally realized I couldn't live with myself anymore. My relationship with Zack was wrong and it was destroying my peace, joy and stability. In Psalm 38, David cried out to God from the depths of his shame:

*O Lord, do not rebuke me in Your wrath,*
*Nor chasten me in Your hot displeasure!*
*For Your arrows pierce me deeply,*
*And Your hand presses me down.*
*There is no soundness in my flesh*
*Because of Your anger,*
*Nor any health in my bones*
*Because of my sin.*
*For my iniquities have gone over my head;*
*Like a heavy burden they are too heavy for me.*
*My wounds are foul and festering*
*Because of my foolishness.*
*I am troubled, I am bowed down greatly;*
*I go mourning all the day long.*
*For my loins are full of inflammation,*
*And there is no soundness in my flesh.*
*I am feeble and severely broken;*
*I groan because of the turmoil of my heart.*
*Lord, all my desire is before You;*
*And my sighing is not hidden from You.*
*My heart pants, my strength fails me;*
*As for the light of my eyes, it also has gone from me.*
*My loved ones and my friends stand aloof from my plague,*
*And my relatives stand afar off...*
*But I, like a deaf man, do not hear;*
*And I am like a mute who does not open his mouth.*
*Thus I am like a man who does not hear,*
*And in whose mouth is no response.*

*For in You, O Lord, I hope;*
*You will hear, O Lord my God.*
*For I said, "Hear me, lest they rejoice over me,*
*Lest, when my foot slips, they exalt themselves against me."*
*For I am ready to fall,*
*And my sorrow is continually before me.*
*For I will declare my iniquity;*
*I will be in anguish over my sin.*
*But my enemies are vigorous, and they are strong;*
*And those who hate me wrongfully have multiplied...*
*Do not forsake me, O Lord;*
*O my God, be not far from me!*
*Make haste to help me,*
*O Lord, my salvation!*

- NKJV

I entrusted a family friend with the knowledge of what was going on so they could give me strength to confront it and deal with the reality of my plight. I knew I had to tell Pastor Bob but I was scared to do so. I felt sick to my stomach as I walked in the back door of the church. I knew this was the only way John and I could possibly have a chance of surviving. I would have to tell the truth out loud. I could not leave Zack on my own. I sat down in Pastor Bob's office and told him everything, asking him to help me put my marriage back together again.

Pastor Bob was quiet and asked how we should tell John. I honestly didn't know how to face him. My heart feared that the Pandora's box I had opened, would not close. Even though I knew the right thing was to stay and work it out, I had no idea where I would put the feelings I had for Zack. "Do you feel like you are in love with him?" Pastor Bob asked.

"Yes, I do," I whispered. The truth of those words had a deep impact. I realized it was now out in the open and it was a shocking revelation, even to me. John was very hurt and furious when he came home from meeting with Pastor Bob. His eyes were blazing, and he had a look and demeanor I had never seen on him before. There were no tears between us. The shallow pool of intimacy we had constructed over the years could not hold the ravenous river of pain now facing us. With few words and a look of disdain that shot through me to the core of my being, he stormed out of the house with a six-pack in his hand (he had never purchased alcohol before during our marriage).

I sat there for a while and contemplated the events that were now in motion unraveling my marriage. This had been the moment I had feared. My sin was revealed and the chips would now fall where they may. I was unexpectedly emotionless. I was surprised by John's fury. Of course, I knew he loved me, but the chasm of passivity and inability to find a soul connection had taken its toll on both of us.

The reality of the situation gave me strength to tell Zack that I couldn't see him anymore. Everything was out in the open and it was over for good between us. I explained that John and I were going to put our life together again. Zack said he didn't believe it and told me he loved me. These words were like a spell cast over my heart; a soul tie that was chained around me.

Pastor Bob felt that with everything that was happening, I needed to go away for a while. The decision was made for me to stay with some friends in the next province over. There was a trucking company that made trips to Alberta and a driver named Glen agreed to take Tyler and me to our friends' home. John walked me to the vehicle to say goodbye and gave me a forced hug. I couldn't bear to look into his eyes.

So much damage had been done in so little time. John was devastated. My parents were beside themselves with confusion and brokenness. At that moment, I realized that a reputation might take a lifetime to build, yet only a moment to destroy. The months that ensued brought with them the most damaging emotional pain that I had ever experienced in my life. I lost my dignity, honor, reputation, veracity and friendships; they were brought down to a heap of rubble.

Glen had a wonderful sense of humor, and while he had no idea what I was going through, he seemed to be aware that I needed a friend. He was one of those "true blue" guys who said what he thought and had the kind of logic you wish political leaders would embody. He helped me pass the time and has remained a friend to this very day.

I will never forget that trip and the long hours of travel in the middle of the night on the quiet open road, alone with my thoughts and fears. There was a sick foreboding that gripped my mind. Now isolated by my actions, I had all the time in the world to think about what I had done. I viewed the past five years on the DVR of my mind's High Definition wide screen.

I walked down the aisle on my wedding day and through the corridors of the years that held such disappointment. I travelled through time, back to the realization of the binding error I had made and the irrevocability of my vows. I reminded God that I had resisted others who had held such strong attractions. Many times I had said 'no' when my flesh said 'yes,' and I walked away when my baser nature told me to stay. I went back farther, to the call of God I had felt on my life as a child and as a teenager. I had begun to speak and teach the Word and to be useful to the Kingdom, but now in my humanity, I believed I had disqualified myself forever. My soul was vexed with anguish.

At about 1 a.m. in the morning, after hours of wrestling with the questions of how I had gotten here and wondering if it would ever be okay again, there was a hushed peace that settled over my spirit as we drove down the dark highway. It was as if the Holy Spirit knew my fleshly being could not take the weight of this brokenness. This breeze of the sweet presence of Jesus brushed over me and caused the emotions that had escaped me during this entire situation to give way. As if a tiny hole in the dam had been carved, I finally cried the tears I could not find during the strain of it all.

The Word of God in Romans chapter eight says that nothing and no one can separate us from the love God. I found this to be true, that not even my deceived, sinful state could cause God to stop loving me. I turned and stared out the window at the darkness and quietly breathed in this much-needed visitation from the Friend who stays closer than a brother. I did not feel I deserved this moment of kindness and compassion from my Holy and Righteous Father.

While in Taber, Alberta, at our friends' home, I tried to figure out what to do. Shame, remorse, confusion, decimation and ruin were now my daily comrades. I could not eat. Caring for Tyler was the only thing that kept me going. The days were long and empty.

My dad came to Alberta to pick me up. We drove all night through a snow storm to get back home. During the trip, he showed me the love of a true father by caring for me in spite of my failure. We talked for hours and I appreciated who he was. He did not try to make me do something I could not do, or force me to agree with his or anyone else's idea of what was right. He just listened and heard my heart about the reality of my plight. It was a conversation that sealed my love for my father. He truly showed me unconditional love and acceptance. He showed me who Jesus was. I had long since believed I had to perform in order to be accepted, yet in this situation I felt I belonged even though my performance had been deplorable.

I was living at my parents' home with Tyler when John told Pastor Bob that he was willing to work this through. I could go home the moment I was willing to commit to this process of healing. But the thought of returning to the awkwardness between us left me emotionless. I did not know how to make the chemistry between John and me work. There was this huge lack of 'something' that we never had.

For some strange reason, veteran Christian radio broadcaster and teacher Chuck Swindoll, had spoken into my life through his program in my most pivotal hours. One night as I drove aimlessly through the streets, I couldn't stop rehashing my situation with John. I was stuck on an endless treadmill of deliberations on which way to go. I had created a nightmare for all of us. I reflected on my choices and how people were horrified at what I had done. I received a few calls from my church friends that weren't too nice and I apologized profusely. I knew my sin; there was no excuse. I also knew I had a life situation that I didn't know how to fix. All I could do was say "sorry," over and over again.

Chuck's words cut me to the core. To the best of my recollection he said, "The sadness in God's heart is when He entrusts leaders with His anointing and they squander it with their immorality and sin. They dishonor the presence of God by disgracing the cause of Christ with their lives of selfishness." That was me. I had done that. I had hurt the name of Jesus, whom I had held up as my Lord and Savior.

I began to sob as he continued, "We need to repent of our sin and return again to our First Love." It was as if Chuck was speaking directly to me and a cast iron wall of failure began to melt under the fire of conviction. I began to cry out, *God change my heart and save me from this mess. I'm so sorry. Please bring me back to the place I once had with You.*

This was the first time that I sensed the strength that comes from true godly sorrow. I asked God to forgive me for the pain I had caused Him and myself. I instantly felt a rush of peace and a knowing in my heart that if God was God, then He could do the impossible and perform a miracle in my life and John's. My heart was filled with an unspeakable calm and I felt the peace I needed to do the right thing. I breathed deeply with my head back on the headrest, knowing I had not been in this place before. It was a tremendous moment.

As courage coursed through my veins, I knew what I had to do. I raced back to my mom and dad's house, and even though it was about

10 p.m., I called John and asked him to please come over right away. I knew I needed to act on this word I felt God had given me to reconcile and trust Him. John had been visiting at his parents' and he asked me why I needed to see him. I responded by saying, "I need to talk to you; it's important, please come."

When John arrived, we went downstairs to talk privately. I noticed that he was distant and cold, but that made sense to me. *Look at what he had been through.* It didn't matter to me now that he was angry; I knew he deserved to be angry. I had this peace inside me that I had not felt in a long time. It was this secure feeling that no matter what, God was with us and He could heal us.

"John, I'm so sorry for what I've done." Tears streamed down my face. "I have no excuse for the pain I've caused you. You've been a wonderful husband and I failed you greatly. I realize tonight that we can make this work. I want to come home." Then I proceeded to tell him about Chuck Swindoll's message and how it had impacted me. I felt a shine in my eyes that had long been gone. The grace of God filled my heart and I had hope that I would devote myself to John and our family and trust God.

John replied, "No, you can't come home. It's over. Are you able to buy me out of our portion of the home with the help of your parents?" I was shocked; surely he wasn't serious? It was too soon to end this and we owed each other one last shot. But he continued, "I went to see a place with my dad today and I can buy it and renovate it. Do you think you can come up with the money before we sell the house? They are looking for a quick sale."

I didn't know what to say. I just stared for a moment in silence. I had not imagined this reaction. Knowing John and his propensity to do the right thing, I thought I would be packing up Tyler and heading home with him that night. "If God is Who He says He is, then there is hope. Can't we put this back together and maybe God would heal what was wrong before?" I said softly. I sat in disbelief as John did not respond as I had hoped. His eyes almost scoffed and his words quickly turned to the logistics of how we might divide the proceeds of the home.

My tears were now completely dried as I stared in confusion. John had told Pastor Bob that if I would be willing to reconcile, he would walk through it with me. But now it was clear, he had set his sights on a new life without me. I didn't really blame him; I had broken all trust and destroyed what little we ever had together. It's just that in the wake of this ruinous event, I was thinking John would at least try for a bit to find a new normal, a new life, possibly a hope that God might use this terrible episode to heal our intimacy. Yes, it seemed like a tall order, but if God is God…

He said, "I'll call you tomorrow and maybe you can ask your parents tonight if they would be willing to help bring closure quickly and pay out my half of the house, otherwise we can just put it up for sale and move on."

I stood silently without the words to further convince him. I knew in my heart there were no words that would fix this. I shut the door as he left and stood there quietly wondering what had just happened. I wish I could say that I was strong, but I wasn't. I was more lost than before. I thought I had a life preserver to hang on to, but clearly that option had deflated and I was now alone again. I was really, *really* alone. If there was no life with John, then what would my future be like?

I had no one at my side. I had lost my friends, church, marriage and home. My family was the only bright spot; the faithful loyalty of blood that remains thicker than water through trials, failures, and crisis. My dad and mom, along with my brother Jeff were kind, even though they all felt sideswiped by life. Everyone liked John and it was a family nightmare that this was over because of me.

My mom and dad could see me wasting away with no appetite in a state of constant depression. A parent's heart is an amazing thing; it's the closest example we have to understanding the heart of Father God. No matter what your kids have done, you love them. No matter the havoc they have wreaked on their own lives that spills over to the entire family, you never stop caring for them.

I thanked God for this one stability. I knew I had embarrassed my missionary family beyond words. I had brought them shame and disgrace. They deserved so much better. I wish that I had been able to see that God loved me no matter what, just like my parents did. But somehow it seemed impossible for me to comprehend that He would ever cast His glance my way again. I had the fleeting moments of feeling His presence softly near me, but it was as if I were a broken clay pot in which the water of God's love just leaked right out. I couldn't contain it; I couldn't keep or maintain the feeling. The shame of my sin was ever before me; I couldn't find reprieve. If John rejected me, I was sure that God also would reject me.

With little to hold on to, I succumbed to the obsession I felt for Zack and resumed the relationship I had paid a very high price to have. Ironically, there was now a deep emptiness; I noted nothing could change. I didn't feel strong inside like I did many years ago. I couldn't find my courage or voice. I didn't feel I deserved much and I became much quieter than the outgoing, vivacious, gregarious girl I once was.

My pastor's wife, Linda, had said as a practicality that I was a lot like Zack and she didn't think our relationship would work. I really didn't understand at the time what she meant, but as the seasons marched on, I soon realized that she was right. Even though I had always been an assertive and high-energy person, Zack's even larger personality began to dominate my world. In hindsight, I am aghast at what I overlooked in the early stages of my obsession.

A voice inside me kept saying something was very wrong. The recent brokenness had shattered my self-esteem and it was very difficult to stand on my own. Soon there were signs of friction in our communication. I had always been able to get my way with John, but I quickly realized it was Zack's way or the highway. Part of me really liked that dynamic because I no longer had to make decisions. Zack just told me how it was.

Life began to get worse. Stress set in my mind and I began waking in the middle of the night with a rush of adrenalin seizing my body. It was as if while sleeping, I could escape to a dream world without pain, but when I woke up, the brutal reality of my situation would grip my mind and send me into a stressful state. For months, I tried to figure out what to do. Shame, remorse, confusion, decimation, and ruin were now my daily comrades.

I received several calls while living with my parents from the friends I had loved and worshiped with at church. They were very honest with me about their concern that Zack was a "vulture" who had taken advantage of me in a vulnerable state. I could not accept that viewpoint. Others were shocked that John had refused my desire to reunite and begged me to give him more time. But I had seen the look in his eyes and heard the tone in his voice; John had made his mind up and I simply didn't feel strong enough to be alone. I wish I had known then what I know now, but life does not give us the lessons first; we must learn them for ourselves—usually the hard way.

# 4

# HARD LESSONS

*Thus says the Lord, your Redeemer, the Holy One of Israel: I am
the Lord your God, Who teaches you to profit, Who leads you in the
way that you should go.*

- Isaiah 48:17

During our conversation, Pastor Bob had brought up another consideration—Zack did not earn much money and could not support a family. At the time, I dismissed Pastor Bob's concerns and just figured it would all work out. I gave little credence to this issue and did not consider the truth that I knew nothing of Zack's work history, ethic, experience or ability.

John and I put the house up for sale and quickly had a buyer. We each came out with enough money for a down payment on a condo. We went to the bank together and sat down with the representative who helped us divide up our cash on hand. When we told the bank representative that we were separating, she commented on how it was nice that we could still be friends. *We were not friends.* I did not know what to call us. It's not as though we were acquaintances; we had been married for five years.

The banker commented on how either one of us could have come at any time and cleaned out the account. We both knew we would never have done that to each other. We received the cash, separated it and closed our joint account. I looked at John and an awkward silence came over us as we moved toward the front door. "Thank you," I said.

John turned to look straight ahead, "Yup, we'll meet to finish up the sale of the house and…" he paused, "that will be it."

"Yes, ok, that will be it." My heart came up to my throat. Indeed this was the end of a significant chapter in my life. It had not gone the way I had expected.

I found a condo in my price range so I had enough money to put down, with enough left over for two months of mortgage payments to get me through until I could find a job. By some form of miracle, I got a job at a steel plant as the receptionist. It was a union job that enabled me to provide for Tyler and me. Things settled down with John and I knew he was a good dad to Tyler. He always paid child support. My heart wept for my little boy who had no choice in how his family had been torn apart. I would cry most days on the way home from work, rehashing in my mind all the steps it had taken to get me into this pathetic, shameful mess.

I tried to make Tyler smile to ease my own pain and we developed this game where I wasn't allowed to finish tucking him in and turn out the light at night until he was laughing really hard. I was glad he could laugh, even though I couldn't remember the last time that I had. I poured myself into him as best I could and would read endless Bible stories, hoping he would learn from them rather than from what life was showing him. Each time I prayed with him, I choked back the tears; this was not the life I wanted to give him.

My relationship with Zack continued and became more and more rocky. We seemed to fight about everything. This was new to me because John and I had such a quiet, respectful relationship. I felt like I was walking on eggshells with Zack. Sales were down at the chemical company where he worked, putting him in a bad mood sometimes.

My energy seemed to be consumed with keeping peace. A few times I swore to myself that I would leave this crazy consuming relationship, but then Zack would apologize for his behavior or blame me. I just didn't have the strength or courage to be alone.

Zack and I had some good times. He could tell the funniest stories. He was also very social so we were able to make new friends at a new church. I was worried that they would find out about our past so I told them. It seemed as if all I ever did was talk about my failures and live with the fear of rejection. As I look back, I am so grateful for some people in this new church who did not push me aside.

Earlier, Pastor Dave Hubert, a well-known and deeply respected local area pastor had called me forward during a Sunday service while I was visiting his church. He knew my family, but didn't know the particulars of my situation. He probably saw me crying throughout the entire worship service so he gathered several people to pray for me at the front. I couldn't contain my sorrow as the power of God flooded over me. A woman said that God was going to form a new way for me in the midst of my storm. It would not be like the past —He had a new day for my life. I cannot describe the joy that filled me as God kindly ministered to me in this way. I didn't feel like I deserved it. I was stunned and humbled.

That day I asked Zack if we could please honor God with our physical relationship and walk in purity. Zack agreed and I was so thankful. Within a few days however, he was angry about our agreement and would not honor my request that we stay abstinent. He said it was as if we were married already so it was ridiculous to abstain. I was too emotionally confused to resist. I was headed for yet another difficult season.

My cousin Velma is also my dear friend. She provided daycare for Tyler while I was at work. She had been such a kind person to me during the whole ordeal. She is the closest thing I have to a sister and she talked me through many long upsetting moments in those difficult years.

After work one day, I picked Tyler up from Velma's house. On this particular day, I walked in the house and gathered my son into my arms with a big hug. As we headed out the door, Velma asked, "How are you doing? Everything ok?"

"Yeah, it's ok," I said, as I gave her a quick look and a smile. But things weren't ok. I was worried because I thought I might be pregnant. I headed straight to the drug store to pick up a pregnancy test, thinking *Dear God, please don't let me be pregnant.* When I got home, I took the pregnancy test. It took approximately five minutes to get the results; they were the longest five minutes of my life. As I sat on the edge of my bed counting the seconds, a terrible feeling gripped my stomach. I thought *No, this can't possibly be. There is no way this could happen, right God?*

As I waited for the pregnancy test to reveal what I already feared in my mind was true, my heart pounded at the staggering fallout this would bring to my life. At that moment, Zack showed up and was overjoyed when he saw what I was doing. *Really?* Our lives were clearly from two totally different paths.

This pregnancy would not mean the same thing to him as it meant to me. His family would have no issue with us having a child out of wedlock. On the other hand, my family would be devastated…again. My legs felt weak as I walked to the bathroom to see the final verdict; the test was indeed pink. *I was pregnant!* I let out a quick gasp. I suddenly saw black fading into my vision, coming from the peripheral corners of my eyes and beginning to close in towards the center. I staggered back to sit down, trying to breathe deeply and slowly. The room began to spin and I knew if I could, I would do anything to take this back. But it was too late.

There were no tears; tears wouldn't change anything. I stared blankly at the wall as thoughts travelled through my head two hundred miles per hour. Once again, I had made decisions that were irrevocable. How could one girl mess one life up so badly? I knew there was a way to get rid of this baby by simply walking into a clinic and having an abortion. That thought came and went quickly. Abortion was not an option for me. I could not go through with a permanent solution to a temporary life crisis.

I knew God loved and cherished every life, regardless of how the conception happened. Psalm 139:13 says, "For You formed my inward parts; You covered me in my mother's womb" (NKJV). God had covered my baby. And I made the choice that she would live.

Velma and her husband, Doug, were gracious and kind. During the next few weeks, Velma courageously walked me through the moments I thought I would never survive. She understood the gravity of my situation. Velma had questioned if I really wanted to continue my relationship with Zack, but once again I felt I had made the bed that I needed to lie in.

I was afraid to tell my parents about the pregnancy. Since I had lost so much weight, I didn't begin to show until over five months had passed. This gave me some time to collect my thoughts and figure out what to do next. I finally had to tell John. He was cold and a little mocking. I asked him if we could please hurry the divorce so I could get married, but he made it clear that he wouldn't cooperate. Zack told my dad about the pregnancy and thankfully bore the brunt of the initial shock waves that hit. My mom was angry, of course, and then sad. I was sad, too.

The stress of everything became overwhelming. Zack and I had chemistry that carried us through but we did not get along. On one particularly bad day, we had a fight so brutal that it broke my heart; the words spoken were so cruel, they left me racing away from my condo with one thought—*I simply could not take life anymore.* Pregnant, alone - really alone – with no friends, no reputation, no life to be proud of and no hope in sight, I sped down the road as it began to rain.

I couldn't stop thinking about how kind John had been to me. Maybe we didn't have that certain magic, but he had been such a nice man. Why didn't he give us one last shot? I found myself in the most desperate state of my life. I did not want to live. I was now with a man who could be punishing and harsh. *This is not the life I hoped for God; this is not what I wanted. I don't want to live; take the pain away, please God. I CAN'T DO IT! Jesus, I just can't do it! Make it better, Jesus…I'm so sorry, I'm so sorry….*

Some of us may severely undervalue our importance in the eyes of our heavenly Father. We have all heard the words of John 3:16, "God so loved the world that He gave His only begotten Son, that whoever believes in Him should not perish but have everlasting life" (NKJV). Why would God allow His very own Son to die a brutal death as the ultimate sacrifice for every one of our sins, if He did not love us extraordinarily? This is such a staggering gift, we quite possibly cannot comprehend it.

Perhaps we cannot comprehend God's gift because we do not value ourselves the way God values us. I struggled for years with this. I would ask God why He cares about us, specks of dust on a planet full of hate and immorality with only a very small portion of people who truly love Him. Why does He care about us? When I took it even further down to just myself, seeing my humanity and my defects, I had to wonder if I could ever be worth His time. He is the Creator of the universe; I am just a broken, sinful girl. Psalm 103:13-14 puts things in perspective: "As a father loves and pities his children, so the Lord loves and pities those who fear Him [with reverence, worship, and awe]. For He knows our frame, He [earnestly] remembers and imprints [on His heart] that we are dust."

I realized that it's *because* we are so minute, fragile, and breakable that He loves us. He created us to be delicate, precious and valuable. The ultimate irony is that in our humanity, He became our Savior and rescued us. Our weaknesses and humanity do not prevent us from entering His throne room; in fact, those very things qualify us for the ultimate price He paid for our redemption.

That day, I cried until I could not cry anymore. I realized there was a little baby in my tummy who didn't ask for any of this, and who certainly deserved to live. I was the one shot she had at life. I started the car and began to drive back home.

Before long, Zack apologized for the fight, but he had a very confusing way of making it seem as if I took everything the wrong way. He was excited that we were going to have a baby and thought we would be a happy family. He never knew how much I had wanted to die that day; he couldn't possibly have understood.

Three months later, Larissa was born and a beautiful breath of fresh air flowed into my life. She was magnificent and she looked right into my eyes as if she had always known me. My precious mom was the first one to the hospital to hold her in the middle of the night. This little baby girl brought laughter and joy to my life that has never left. When Tyler came to the hospital, you could see the quiet awe on his face. He was uncharacteristically gentle and quiet and we had a new and unexpected kind of family. I hovered over my children and prayed that God would heal us and bring peace.

At the end of 1993, Zach and I were married by a wonderful clergyman, Pastor Syd Lowndes. He took pity on our situation and blessed us with a church wedding. I thank God for this man who showed the mercy and grace of God to us. He did not reject us, but instead he became the very hands of Jesus extended to the broken. My heart was so grateful for such a true act of kindness.

Finally we were a legal, proper family. I was so relieved that I could simply begin a new life. I asked God to forgive me over and over again. I promised that I would make this marriage work and this time there would be no divorce. I would work this out at any cost. Although there were a couple of police incidents in the early years, we kept working through it. We went to counseling, tried to learn communication skills, and just kept on going. I was determined not to lose my newfound dignity ever again.

Life passed quickly and we had another baby. Aaron became the final incredible addition to my life. I was blessed again to have a calm, quiet boy who liked to sleep. From the moment he was born, he was a delight. Before I was pregnant with him, my dad said that adding another child to this equation was going to complicate it, but I told him, "There is a child inside of me that must be born. He's meant to be here and is begging me to let him live." Now Aaron was here and I couldn't resist picking him up, snuggling, tickling and chasing him through the house, as his laughter chimed out. Carl Sandburg once said, "A baby is God's opinion that the world should go on."

I loved my children deeply but I missed the joy I once had in my own soul many long years before. My heart was still full of shame and pain from all that had happened. Try as I might, I could not shake the sadness that set in for several years. The dreams of the little missionary girl from Africa to be used by God faded into the distance.

I was completely disqualified, diminished and destroyed. The enemy told me over and over that I would never rise out of these ashes. Regret was my daily companion combined with an overwhelming sadness that the gifts and calling of God had been demolished by my foolish and self-destructive choices. There seemed to be no hope for redemption; no recovery could possibly be made from such desperately imprudent decisions. How could God ever fix this mess? The silence was deafening and I could not conceive any possible answers or solutions to my pain, shame and regret.

I was being lied to and my mind was being tossed around with worry and anxiety. The Word of God says in 2 Corinthians 10:5, "We demolish arguments and every pretension that sets itself up against the knowledge of God, and we take captive every thought to make it obedient to Christ" (NIV). I was ashamed of my own failures and didn't feel worthy to come before God. Even though Psalm 103:12 clearly should have released me of my despair - "As far as the east is from the west, so far He has removed our transgressions from us" (NKJV) - I still felt guilty. I lacked the faith to take God at His Word.

The enemy's tactics have not changed in thousands of years. He tries to confuse us, offers counterfeit gods, false rituals and remedies to our pain that do not lead to healing, but rather to destruction. He lies, steals and manipulates our minds. The solution is Jesus. He is our Healer, Redeemer, Peace, and the One True God who, since the dawn of time, has been the only answer to mankind's hurting hearts. I knew this in my head but the truth of it had never reached my heart.

A routine Wednesday evening radically changed my life. I debated if I should go to the mid-week service or not. By sheer force of will, I put my shoes on and headed to Glad Tidings Church. Pastor Culley brought in a life-size cross that was old and rugged. I glanced at it quickly and sat down with no expectation or understanding of the magnitude of power that was about to be revealed to me that evening.

I knew all about what Jesus had done on the cross. My mom had taught me about that in Sunday school with a little booklet when I was just a child. The booklet had a black page that represented sin, a red page that represented the blood of Jesus, and a white page that represented how we are forgiven and then made white as snow. My dad had given his best years to preaching about the cross. But somehow, for this ruined, fragmented woman, there was no remedy in this truth. I had carved out the consequences of my journey—one bad mistake after another.

Annoyingly, Pastor Culley asked everyone to write down the three sins that had plagued them and nail them to the cross. This was bothersome to me because I didn't want to think about my sins, I didn't want to write them down, and I didn't want to see them on a paper in front of me. I wanted to forget about my sins. I thought that someone might even try to read everyone's sins from these papers after we all went home.

This seemed to be such a ridiculous exercise. It made me angry. *Manipulation,* I thought, *I'm not doing it!* The entire congregation began to line up with their little papers containing the sins they would carry to the cross. Soon I realized that I would be the only one sitting in the pews if I didn't participate—then I would have to add 'rebellion' as one of my sins!

So, as small and illegibly as I could, I wrote my sins down right in the middle of the paper so I could fold it in four and put the nail right through the middle. I knew Jesus knew exactly what my sins were and as I looked around, I realized that probably most of the people in the room also knew my failures. My family had been fairly well known so it had not gone unnoticed that their daughter had fallen.

God alone would read these sins. They had stolen everything from me: my peace, my joy, my dignity, my destiny, and my world. Reluctantly, I shuffled into the line-up. I knew the songs they were singing. I had known them my whole life. *"Oh, the blood of Jesus, that washes white as snow…It reaches to the highest mountain, it flows to the lowest valley… it will never lose it's power."*

I knew Jesus had died for my sins—the ones I held in my hands that had ruined my life. As the worship leader began to sing, *"On a hill far away stood an old rugged cross, the emblem of suffering and shame…,"* I knew my own self-inflicted suffering and shame had been beyond debilitating and I believed that nothing could change it.

The words continued, *"…How I love that old cross, where the dearest and best, for a world of lost sinners was slain. So I'll cherish the old rugged cross, till my trophies at last I lay down…"* I had no trophies. Tears began to stream down my face. It had not worked; the cross had not healed me. My life was in an unbearable state of ruin. So much was lost; such unbelievable sorrow and remorse had seized me. *Jesus, I'm so broken.*

There are three specific times in my life when the Holy Spirit spoke into my heart so powerfully that it changed the course of my life from that day forward. This was the first one. It was at this moment that the Holy Spirit whispered a deafening, yet completely silent series of questions into my being. "Was it not enough for you? What Jesus did; was it not enough to cover your sin? Must He die again so you will receive the gift of forgiveness?"

I stopped dead in my tracks as the line-up continued toward the cross. That was a terrible, staggering, confounding question: *Must He die again so I could receive His forgiveness?* I looked up at that rugged cross on the platform. It was as if I saw His bloodied body, His ravaged skin, the crown of thorns, and the gash in His side with water and blood gushing out, as His life was giving way to death. Isaiah 52:14 (NKJV) says, "So His visage was marred more than any man, and His form more than the sons of men."

Jesus never deserved one moment of agony. It was my depravity, iniquity and wickedness that caused this price to be required by a Holy God. How could I be so arrogant as to negate, diminish, and nullify this magnificent gift that was given on my behalf by the One Who was blameless? For the first time in my miserable journey of failure, I realized that the price had already been paid for my freedom.

Redemption had come a long, long time ago, yet in my self-centered world I could not receive it. In reality, I had rejected it. I had believed the lie that I would have to pay the penalty for what I had done. Suddenly, the clarity and magnificence of the power of the cross flooded not only my mind, but also my spirit. If I would just receive this free vindication for all I had done, I would be completely released. It was so simple that I had not seen it. In spite of my knowledge of the Word and the truth since my childhood, it had escaped me. I had not trusted God with my humanity.

Pastor Culley later said he had to turn around to see who was pulverizing the nail with the hammer so loudly. I took aim and repeatedly pounded that nail into the cross and truly received what Jesus did for me for the first time in my whole life. The awesome price had been paid and this was the last day that I would let the enemy tell me that it was not enough! I hit the nail over and over again.

I was angry at the devil for lying to me; I should have been free years ago.

It was all I could do to remain standing and not fall to the foot of the cross and hold on to it for dear life. I put my hand on the cross and touched the grace that had always been there. I felt its power. I wiped my tears away with a new resolve and determination. The heaviness of this revelation was overpowering. I walked slowly back to my seat as if I had lead weights in my shoes. I was undone with the gravity and magnitude of this disclosure. Overcome, I left that night knowing I would NEVER be the same!

What I truly didn't understand was how exciting this journey was going to get. With this profound truth alive in my heart, God was going to unleash an adventure so amazing, it could only be orchestrated by Him. His relentless redemption had pursued and captured my soul and it was going to transform my destiny!

# 5

# RAGS TO RICHES

*But now [in spite of past judgments for Israel's sins], thus says the Lord, He Who created you, O Jacob, and He Who formed you, O Israel: Fear not, for I have redeemed you [ransomed you by paying a price instead of leaving you captives]; I have called you by your name; you are Mine.*

- Isaiah 43:1

God gave me a picture to illustrate His love for us. It was a picture of a huge flea market full of useless, damaged and broken items. There were torn lampshades, dented pots, tables and chairs with missing legs, and a whole lot of junk that nobody wanted to buy. I knew those items represented all of us in our tarnished state, discarded and disqualified----all the dreams that would never be realized.

In that picture, I also saw a man who looked wealthy and powerful. He had an entourage of men in white overalls following him. This affluent man began to go through table after table of refuse and scrap. He picked up one piece, examined it carefully, and then put it back down. Onlookers were suddenly stunned when he said, "I'll take it all…every wrecked, fragmented, cracked and ruined piece----I will take it all!" He offered a price that was way too high so the merchants quickly agreed.

The men in the white overalls began to load it all up. There was a woman standing nearby who softly asked the man why he would take all this broken junk? "Ah," said the gracious man, "I am a restorer. I redeem items whose value others have overlooked. They may be in ruin today, but by tomorrow you won't recognize them." Isaiah 58:12 says, "And your ancient ruins shall be rebuilt; you shall raise up the foundations of [buildings that have laid waste for] many generations; and you shall be called Repairer of the Breach, Restorer of Streets to Dwell In."

In the Bible, God called a man named Nehemiah, who was a cup-bearer to the king, to go back to Jerusalem and rebuild the walls of the city that had been destroyed. His heart was broken because the sins of Israel had caused such carnage. He wept before God, asking Him to forgive the people and to remember His promises to them. The walls were destroyed seemingly beyond repair, but God granted Nehemiah's request.

The task was daunting to the point that it almost seemed impossible. Enemies in the area scoffed at the work being done. In Nehemiah 4:2 they said, "Can they bring the stones back to life from those heaps of rubble—burned as they are?" (NIV). But Nehemiah knew that God was a miracle working God and he answered them by saying, "The God of heaven will give us success."

In our own lives, we may have experienced such failure that there are mockers who just laugh when they see us attempt to repair the damage. But the Word of God says that He brings beauty for ashes and the oil of joy for mourning (Isaiah 61:3). God's eyes are on those who are broken-hearted and those who cannot be fixed.

In Nehemiah's day, God provided the new wood and iron for the gates that needed repair. He also took the rubble and stones that had been burned, along with the trash and junk that had been tossed aside and deemed useless. From this, He incorporated those parts that had been heated in the fire and made strong right back into the wall—nothing was wasted.

He does the same thing in our lives. He takes our discarded parts that were destroyed by the enemy's siege on our souls, parts that were tried in the fire of adversity, and brings a new season in our lives, rebuilding the path we were intended to walk. Yes, the path may look a little different as those burned up stones now add character to our journey, but the restored foundation will stand as a marvelous tribute to the glory of God. It will be for our naysayers as it was for those who had once mocked Nehemiah's journey: "When all our enemies heard about this, all the surrounding nations were afraid and lost their self-confidence, because they realized that this work had been done with the help of our God" (Nehemiah 6:16, NIV).

When God takes your mess, your ancient ruins and rubble, others will stand in quiet disbelief knowing that truly an incredible work of God had to take place for your dead bones to walk again. God doesn't waste anything—the pain or shame or the mistakes or failures of our past or future. None of it will be worthless.

Sometimes we may think that ours is just too big of a mess for God to fix. It may seem like all has been lost and we find ourselves feeling empty, broken and disqualified. We may even look back at better years and wonder what happened— where it all went wrong. It may seem as if the walls of our existence have been destroyed and we have nothing left. But God is the creative force that put the very universe in place and He is a master at making masterpieces out of mistakes.

The next few days after my cross experience were like sunshine after a cold and bitter storm. There was an incredible peace that enveloped me and I found myself singing around the house for the first time in years. I felt like Job when he said in Job 33:28, "God has delivered me from going down to the pit, and I shall live to enjoy the light of life" (NIV). I knew I had changed, but I also knew that my outward circumstances had not. Life would get much worse before it got better.

The fear, resentment and sheer powerlessness I felt in trying to make someone else be nice to me, love me, or not be angry with me was so tiresome and debilitating. I recalled a time during the first two years of my marriage to Zack when he had said words that had cut me to the core of my being. I felt so hurt, defenseless, belittled, and distraught over our relationship, had I known a gun was available to me at that very moment, I truly believe I would have used it against him.

It terrified me that my emotions were in such chaos and so out of balance that I would even entertain such a thought. I was a mess and I could not handle the rejection I felt from Zack. On another occasion, he became very angry and threw my clothes over the balcony of our condo. I called my cousin Velma and again she questioned if I really wanted to continue in this relationship. Of course I did. "I have to," I told her.

Zack and I had been going to a series of different counselors to get help for our marriage. We had individual and couples sessions. During these sessions, I learned so much about myself. I also gained some good insight into the post-traumatic stress I had experienced. It was as if I had been driving a nice car (representing my life) and had crashed it into a wall. I survived the crash, but I was driving with a severely mangled frame. Nevertheless, I knew God was re-aligning my foundation.

The journey seemed so long and taxing. I tried many different approaches to make things better with Zack. I yelled back; I was silent. I cried; I became angry. I tried whatever I thought would save our marriage. Zack would say, "I'm the boss," and he definitely wanted things his way. Many things were difficult, but I didn't want to go through a second divorce because the first one had been so debilitating. I didn't want to go down that road again.

I remember a key moment with one of the counselors as I explained how abandoned I felt when Zack would leave the house while we were in the middle of sorting an argument out. The counselor asked me, "Why do you choose to see it that way?" I looked at him as if to say, *How else would I see it?* He just sat there quietly as I pondered the question again. *Why do I choose to see it that way?* I was baffled by the query and had to ask myself, *What are some other ways to see the exact same situation?*

I was being forced to think outside of the box that I had created in my own mind. When Zack left in anger, I felt alone and rejected. The counselor said, "Maybe he needs to cool off; maybe his leaving is safer for you or it might be that Zack knows it bothers you when he leaves so he keeps doing it." I thought long and hard for a few days over this eye-opener.

Choosing how I would frame a situation in my mind and how I would respond was a gigantic change in the way I dealt with Zack and every other area of my life. What if I actually chose to enjoy the peace and quiet of the house, watch a good movie, read a book, etc.? Stepping away from my routine thought patterns and "wounded-spirit" mentality took some time, but I began to retrain my mind to walk in *redemption*, rather than *rejection*.

I realized that even Jesus was repeatedly attacked in regard to His identity. In Matthew 4, the devil kept saying, "If you are the Son of God…" Jesus always answered him with scripture. The Holy Spirit had revealed so powerfully what Jesus did for me out of sheer love and devotion—one broken sinful girl. Why would I believe one more lie from the enemy?

I began to apply the Word of God to every problem we had. If Zack was angry with me, I stopped and thought about what that really meant. Did it mean that I was deserving of that anger? No, in fact Proverbs 29:22 (NIV) says, "An angry person stirs up conflict, and a hot-tempered person commits many sins." Furthermore, Proverbs 22:24 states, "Make no friendship with an angry man, And with a furious man do not go" (NKJV).

According to Romans 4:7, I was a forgiven and blessed child of God: "Blessed are those whose transgressions are forgiven, whose sins are covered" (NIV). Did this mean that I had to defend myself or be angry? No, Jesus stood in the gap and defended me before the Father and paid a price I could not pay so I could stand in strength and dignity. First John 2:1 says, "My dear children, I write this to you so that you will not sin. But if anybody does sin, we have an advocate with the Father—Jesus Christ, the Righteous One."

I began to answer every one of my doubts and long-held beliefs with a new and powerful Word from God. I devoured the Scriptures, looking for answers that I had never embraced or seen before. When I was afraid, verses like Psalm 27:5 came to mind: "For in the day of trouble he will keep me safe in his dwelling; he will hide me in the shelter of his sacred tent and set me high upon a rock" (NIV).

When I felt attacked, I would recall Isaiah 54:17: "'No weapon formed against you shall prosper, and every tongue which rises against you in judgment you shall condemn. This is the heritage of the servants of the LORD, and their righteousness is from Me,' says the LORD" (NKJV). When I felt like Zack was stonewalling or would not respond to me during an argument, I knew God heard me. Psalm 55:17 states, "Evening, morning and noon I cry out in distress, and he hears my voice." (NIV).

Romans 8:31-39 became my stronghold:

*"What then shall we say to these things? If God is for us, who can be against us? He who did not spare His own Son, but delivered Him up for us all, how shall He not with Him also freely give us all things? Who shall bring a charge against God's elect? It is God who justifies. Who is he who condemns? It is Christ who died, and furthermore is also risen, who is even at the right hand of God,*

*who also makes intercession for us. Who shall separate us from the love of Christ? Shall tribulation, or distress, or persecution, or famine, or nakedness, or peril, or sword?...Yet in all these things we are more than conquerors through Him who loved us. For I am persuaded that neither death nor life, nor angels nor principalities nor powers, nor things present nor things to come, nor height nor depth, nor any other created thing, shall be able to separate us from the love of God which is in Christ Jesus our Lord."*

It is so easy to gloss over these well-known scriptures, but it is powerful to dissect every word slowly and to breathe in the magnitude of it. Corrie ten Boom once said, "You may never know that Jesus is all you need until Jesus is all you have." I only had Jesus left. The Word of God became my lifeline to sanity, peace and security.

I was set free daily by the simplicity of *truth*. I began to release the fear of being rejected, abandoned and misunderstood. I became far less affected by criticism, controlling statements and the basic human fear of being alone. I wrote scriptures out in my notebooks and sometimes taped them to my mirror in the bathroom. These scriptures began to wash over my soul and I realized that I was healing month-by-month and year-by-year. I trusted God to carry me through the darkness and He was about to give me a huge insight into who I truly was in His eyes.

Prior to my journey to the cross, I had disqualified myself and decided whatever God's perfect plan had been certainly couldn't happen now that I had ruined my life. I had been under the wrong assumption that I had to be *perfect* in order to fulfill His perfect will.

Since that was impossible, I gave up on believing I could do anything great for God. I was content to simply eat the crumbs that might happen to fall under the table of God's blessing. I felt like the crumbs were all I deserved, so I accepted them.

In the Gospel of Luke there is a parable I which the Master invited everyone to a banquet but no one came because they had some excuse or another or were too busy. My problem was not being too busy; I just didn't think I was invited. In Luke 14:21, the Great Master told His servant, "Go out quickly into the streets and alleys of the town and bring in the poor, the crippled, the blind and the lame"(NIV). I was very lame and broken from my wayward ways, yet I had difficulty understanding that this invitation was given to me—to come and eat at His table. I was content to eat the scraps that fell under the table, but God showed me that I was His daughter—a princess invited to dine with her Father.

Understanding my position in Christ after such failure continued to be a process. I knew that I was free from my shame because of what Jesus did on the cross, but it was still difficult to find my new identity. I had to transform my thinking about who I really was. It was on this journey of finding my heritage in God alone that I attended a regular session with our marriage counselor, Dave. This would be the second time that God spoke so strongly to my heart—changing me forever!

Dave asked me to envision myself standing before God himself and to describe what it looked like. The immediate picture that came to my mind was of me standing in a huge room with a light shining down on me, which I perceived to be God's presence. I was wearing a blue hospital gown, the kind that opens at the back.

This was how I saw myself—as a person who obviously was in recovery, but still sick. I described the scene to Dave and he prayed and asked God to supernaturally show me how He saw me. Instantly, it was as if I could see myself from a camera circling about my body. As the view moved steadily around me, every part of me changed.

I was suddenly in a spectacular white dress made of satin with diamonds, jewels, and pearls embedded throughout. I had sparkling earrings and a gorgeous necklace of diamonds and pearls. As the picture continued to be revealed, I saw that my face shone with an incredible light and there was a magnificent shimmering crown on my head.

It was a picture of radiant brilliance. I thought at the time, that it looked as if I were a bride. It staggered me because I knew the Holy Spirit was revealing to me how the Lord saw me, but the image was so far from how I saw myself. I became a sobbing mess as I realized God saw me as an exquisite, beautiful woman of royal heritage, adorned in stunning apparel.

I tried to explain this to Dave but I was left speechless after this vision. There were no adequate words to describe it. Since he was a man who knew God had met many of his clients in their broken places and had impacted them during prayer, all he could say was "Isn't God amazing?" I nodded my head with a grateful smile and went home knowing that I was not who *I* thought I was or who *others* thought I was—I was truly who *God* thought I was!

Whether I had known it before that moment or not did not change the fact that I was created to be royalty. I had a position of power, yet I had been walking around as a pauper. Later as I studied what the Bible says about how God sees us, I realized He had shown me an accurate picture of His view of me. Psalm 8:5 says, "You have made man a little lower than the angels and crowned them with glory and honor" (NIV). I pondered and read it again and again out loud, *Crowned with glory and honor.* And then I read in Isaiah 61:10, "He has covered me with the robe of righteousness, as a bridegroom decks himself with a garland, and as a bride adorns herself with her jewels."

That's how God sees me—like a bride prepared for her wedding day in astonishing fashion: beautified and dignified with jewels. He doesn't see us the way we see ourselves - all messed up and messed over. To our Father, we are a beautiful bride, a wonderful creation, born for great purpose and made to have dominion in this lifetime. The enemy wants to convince us that we're done in and there's no hope for us, that we are disqualified and used up. But that's a lie!

There were two separate times during this period when two different people prayed these words over me in a short period of time: *You are a queen before the Lord.* I thought that was a strange way to put it. It seemed a little egotistical, if not ridiculous, to say that I was a queen before the Lord. It was disconcerting and I couldn't really believe these women could have the mind of the Lord when they prayed these words. It didn't seem right, proper or even humble to think this of myself. I thought it was odd that two times the exact same thing was said to me. What was God saying—if anything? Was there any truth to these strange words concerning where my identity lay in Christ?

I found this passage that reveals how God expressed His adoration and love to Jerusalem—His bride. It says in Ezekiel 16:9-14, "I bathed you with water and washed the blood from you and put ointments on you. I clothed you with an embroidered dress and put sandals of fine leather on you. I dressed you in fine linen and covered you with costly garments. I adorned you with jewelry: I put bracelets on your arms and a necklace around your neck, and I put a ring on your nose, earrings on your ears and a beautiful crown on your head. So you were adorned with gold and silver; your clothes were of fine linen and costly fabric and embroidered cloth. Your food was honey, olive oil and the finest flour. You became very beautiful and rose to be a queen. And your fame spread among the nations on account of your beauty, because the splendor I had given you made your beauty perfect, declares the Sovereign LORD" (NIV).

I couldn't believe how God described the city that represented the people He loved...*You became very beautiful and rose to be a queen.* Could I dare to believe God would remove the stain so far from me that I could walk into a destiny this glorious—to be a queen before the Lord? That seemed way too far-fetched for one such as myself, knowing where I came from.

According to Revelation 21:2-3, we are the New Jerusalem and we are prepared and adorned as a bride: "And I saw the holy city, the new Jerusalem, descending out of heaven from God, all arrayed like a bride beautified and adorned for her husband; then I heard a mighty voice from the throne and I perceived its distinct words, saying, See! The abode of God is with men, and He will live (encamp, tent) among them; and they shall be His people, and God shall personally be with them and be their God."

Wow! This was profound - our identity in Christ is of epic proportions. There is nothing noble in pity, nothing of greatness in insecurity, nothing wise in not knowing who you are, nothing priceless about thinking you are worthless, nothing astonishing about being unaware or your intrinsic value, and nothing profound about underestimating and under utilizing your talent. God made you for a magnificent purpose. Walk in your call and destiny.

I recently spoke at a recovery house and again, as always, I was so inspired by the stories of those who were fighting to beat the demons of addiction. You are not your addiction, you are not your failure, you are not your shame, and you are not even your incredible successes. You are God's child—created to embrace Him as Daddy. He takes your 'stuff' in exchange for His power.

*Feeling disqualified?* Don't believe it! *Feeling rejected?* Don't embrace it! *Feeling despair?* Don't accept it! *Feeling sad?* Don't receive it! *Feeling alone?* Don't trust it! Trust in *truth*, not in feelings. The truth is you are royalty, qualified, received, and entitled to joy, hope and redemption.

To everyone who has been rejected, to all who have felt the sting of abandonment, for those who were not invited to the party—I have a crazy offer for you! You are distinctly and personally invited to become royalty: adopted into God's family, a son or daughter of the King of kings, given full rights to the inheritance, power, and family name. John 1:12 (NIV) says, "Yet to all who did receive him, to those who believed in his name, he gave the right to become children of God."

Ephesians 1:4-5 reminds us, "In love he predestined us for adoption to sonship through Jesus Christ" (NIV). Stand tall and walk in your call!

God has given each one of us the keys to elevate us out of darkness, decay and sin, into a royal providential position so powerful that we are left speechless and in awe. What God has designed for His kids is almost unbelievable. It takes intimacy, faith, knowledge of the Word, and confidence in who God is to know who we are.

I recently shared a thought that God dropped in my heart. Many of us like to see what the young princes in England are up to: their growing years, love affairs, weddings, successes and failures are all splashed around the globe on the front covers of the tabloids. Ponder for a moment on some of the most negative press that you can remember about either Prince William or Prince Harry. Perhaps it was a crude night out on the town captured by the paparazzi for all to see or the rumors circulated that left mothers around the world shaking their heads in disgust. I'm sure the queen was so mortified she couldn't even enjoy her afternoon tea. Answer this one question though, *Were both of them still princes the next day?* The answer of course is 'yes.' Likewise, we are still royalty even when we have *royally* messed up!

# 6

# NEW CREATION

*Thus says the Lord, the Redeemer of Israel, Israel's Holy One, to him whom man rejects and despises, to him whom the nations abhor, to the servant of rulers: Kings shall see you and arise; princes, and they shall prostrate themselves, because of the Lord, Who is faithful, the Holy One of Israel, Who has chosen you.*

- Isaiah 49:7

God is not surprised by your life today. He is not shocked and mortified by what you have done. He knew what you would do before you did it and He has already determined in His heart to forgive you when you repent because of what Jesus did as your advocate on the cross. I began to truly embrace my destiny as God's daughter. It didn't matter what I had done; God forgave me. It didn't matter that life was still imperfect and marked with consequences; He was with me. It didn't even matter that I couldn't see a true ending to the difficulties; I was His heir to the throne of grace and that's all I needed to be.

Finding my identity in Christ began to change everything about my perspective and behavior. Jesus specifically chose people who showed an extreme ability to fail and miss the mark. He saw those who would bow in great sorrow and repentance. He knew beforehand that they were imperfect and in need of a Savior.

Consider the story of Peter, who denied knowing Jesus just before He was crucified. Matthew 26:31 tells that Jesus knew in advance that His disciples, specifically Peter, would betray him. "Then Jesus told them, 'This very night you will all fall away on account of me, for it is written, "I will strike the shepherd, and the sheep of the flock will be scattered""" (NIV).

In verse 33, Peter indignantly replied, "Even if all fall away on account of you, I never will" (NIV). But Jesus knew how Peter would fail and He said to him, "Truly I tell you,… this very night, before the rooster crows, you will disown me three times" (Matthew 26:34, NIV). The disciples had no idea that within a few hours of Jesus speaking this, He would be arrested and that fatal night would begin its destined end leading to the cross.

As Jesus was led away by the guards, Peter found himself alone and frightened by all that was happening. As the evening wore on, people began to recognize him as the one who was always with Jesus. By the time the third person accused him, Matthew 26:74-75 tells us, "He (Peter) began to call down curses, and he swore to them, 'I don't know the man!' Immediately a rooster crowed. Then Peter remembered the word Jesus had spoken, 'Before the rooster crows, you will disown me three times.' And he went outside and wept bitterly" (NIV).

Significant personal growth came about when I was no longer afraid of others' anger and judgments. Since I was a little girl, I hated the feeling I got when I thought someone was angry with me. This would strike fear in my heart even as an adult. I didn't want anyone to be angry. That's why I would go to great lengths to dissuade Zack's anger. If that didn't work, I would get angry in return and things would begin to escalate.

I finally realized that nothing worked to bring peace to our relationship. I began to understand that I could not change Zack and that I was not responsible for his anger, behavior or judgments. There was little I could do—except pray and walk in my own peace from the Lord. I actually became comfortable with Zack being angry and did not react to it any longer.

I asked God to take Zack's heart of stone and turn it into a heart of flesh. It became very clear that even God is bound by the free will He gave to mankind. God does not force anyone to love, honor or serve Him. It is always man's choice. Free will was the ultimate gift God gave mankind—the right to choose to love Him, believe or not believe in Him, reject Him, hate Him, or embrace Him. We can be so angry at God when something terrible happens because of another man's choice to do evil. However, if we did not have this cherished gift of freedom, we would simply be robots forced to serve Him.

It is illogical to blame God for the choice wicked men make to do heinous acts when we treasure our personal right to decide our own fate. God will not take this authority from us because He doesn't want androids. He wants friends who will choose to make Him their Lord. It was a definitive, calculated risk God took to give away a power that only He had—freedom of choice—to find those willing to truly love Him by their own hearts desire.

Our free will is what makes us supreme and dominant over all other creations. Our success is not dependent on our brains, beauty, family, origin, education, charisma, fierce determination or discipline. It is dependent on us choosing God and His master plan for our lives. My acceptance of the fact that I was powerless to change anyone else brought about a new freedom for me. I realized that I was not responsible for Zack's behavior, mood or anger. That was between him and God and that's where I left it. In as much as I could, I would live at peace with Zack and not take things personally.

One day he became furious that I had bought a grocery item we already had in the pantry. He began yelling and soon became livid. We went into the living room where I stood looking at him. I told him I was sorry and it was an oversight. He waved his arms around and was very upset. I thought about how hard it must be for him to carry around all this anger about such small things. *What would it be like to live with all that frustration?*

My heart was settled within me and I knew I did not need to feel any condemnation over his accusation. It was a small thing to have purchased something we didn't need, so I simply held my peace. I would not receive his anger into my being; I simply stood there calmly. As I silently observed him, I suddenly had a sense that something had cloaked itself around me in protection and I felt warmth on my back.

I actually became unaware at this point of what Zack was saying. I had this strong feeling that I was not standing alone. I sensed that there were angels standing on guard beside me. As something warm continued across my back, I had an inner knowing that I was being supernaturally protected. I realized that in releasing all the anger and retribution from my heart, I had paved the way for God to stand in my defense. It felt as though there was someone beside me who was at least twice as large as I was.

This incident gave me insight into the spiritual war that goes on around us. Ephesians 6:12 says, "For we do not wrestle against flesh and blood, but against principalities, against powers, against the rulers of the darkness of this age, against spiritual hosts of wickedness in the heavenly places" (NKJV). This insight me the strength I needed to keep forgiving, to walk in serenity, and let God be my Defender.

Sometimes the air in our home would be so thick with tension that inevitably a huge fight would follow. At times Zack would bump up against me with his chest and say, "Remember, it's till death do us part." I would feel a cold shiver go through my body and that scared me. Later Zack would seem sorry for his ways and would make it up to me by being overly nice and kind. It was like I could breathe again. This cycle was continuous.

During one of these cycles, things got especially bad. There had been a string of days of criticism, bad moods and anger. The realization that I couldn't change anything by my response or lack of response was sinking in. I knew the only possible solution was to separate and give each of us some time to re-evaluate our positions. I didn't want to live like this anymore, but I didn't want to give up. *And I certainly did not want to go through another divorce!*

I asked Zack to agree to some time apart, but he wouldn't. He flippantly said I could leave if I wanted to. I felt extremely powerless and had no idea how to change things. My pastor was particularly skilled in dealing with these situations so he met with us and asked Zack to respect my wishes for a separation. I prayed that Zack would accept it and to my amazement he did. It was a miracle when Zack reluctantly said he would go.

It took about three weeks of separation and Zack became a changed man, or so it seemed. He had no anger or criticism; he was in a great mood. I had seen this side of him before and knew that things could go dark again, but I really wanted to keep moving forward in a positive direction, and most of all, I did not want another failure to deal with. My dad once told me to minimize the negatives and accentuate the positives. This was good advice for marriage. At least when Zack was in this place of cooperation, it made things easier. We reconciled and I remember telling my pastor's wife, "I think our relationship is finally going to be healed."

I was no longer awakened at night by those terrible adrenalin rushes. I marveled that I was in a new place emotionally, physically and spiritually. The scriptures I was inhaling were breathing life and light into my spirit. Zack and I seemed to have fewer quarrels for a season—but we also had less interaction overall. It wasn't long before I began to see his old self returning, but I didn't take it personally like I used to. It was a different kind of living.

My heart was at peace with the journey. I truly hoped God would be able to use my life to do a great work but I was content to live a simple life being a mom, wife and homemaker. Those things consumed my days. The Bible says godliness with contentment is great gain (1 Timothy 6:6). I felt like I had gained a mind of serenity by completely trusting God for every step, in spite of my ongoing difficult circumstances.

I noticed that when I saw or heard a speaker who had an inspired and anointed word from God, there would be a fire in my belly. I physically felt warmth or churning in my stomach. This brought an overwhelming desire to share the Word, which would then be followed by a great sadness. I would think, *I can't do that. I'm divorced and have not lived a life worthy of God's call.*

I caught myself making judgments and assumptions once again, thinking God could not use me because of my failures rather than living in the relentless redemption of Jesus through the power of the cross. I compared myself with the "perfect-looking people" like those with only one marriage, a powerful ministry, or a great career. The Bible says that all have sinned and fall short of the glory of God (Romans 3:23); whether it is a public failure or a private sin, we are all imperfect. In fact, according to Isaiah 64:6, our righteousness is as filthy rags.

I took great comfort from the story in John 8 about the woman who was caught in adultery and brought before the town. Jesus stooped down and wrote in the sand, as though He could not hear what the scribes and Pharisees were saying as they continued to try to trap Him with their accusations. John 8:7-11 says, "He raised Himself up and said to them, 'He who is without sin among you, let him throw a stone at her first.' And again He stooped down and wrote on the ground. Then those who heard it, being convicted by their conscience, went out one by one, beginning with the oldest even to the last. And Jesus was left alone, and the woman standing in the midst. When Jesus had raised Himself up and saw no one but the woman, He said to her, 'Woman, where are those accusers of yours? Has no one condemned you?' She said, 'No one, Lord.' And Jesus said to her, 'Neither do I condemn you; go and sin no more.' Then Jesus spoke to them again, saying, 'I am the light of the world. He who follows Me shall not walk in darkness, but have the light of life'" (NKJV).

When Jesus declared to that shattered woman that if she would follow Him, she would not walk in darkness but have the light of life, it gave me hope that my life could be full of His brightness, purpose and favor. It was still hard to see this truth at times, but healing a wound takes time and ointment. The Word of God became my ointment and I could slowly and steadily see that Jesus was healing me.

We hadn't been able to afford much at the time, so Zack decided to start his own business by opening a computer store. I supported his dream by signing on the dotted line with creditors using our house as collateral. My parents had lent me a substantial amount of money to help purchase the house after we sold my condo. Zack had no assets when we got married.

I willingly and wholeheartedly wanted to stand with him as he tried to get his career off the ground. I truly believed he could sell snow to polar bears, so I backed him all the way in his pursuit. He really had a gift in sales. But even so, business was not good; it was a constant struggle. There were little miracles that seemed to give us just enough to get by, but overall we were going in the hole month after month.

One time, Zack was at the church fixing a computer and he came home with a wrapped roast ham from the food bank. We were so broke that I actually had tears in my eyes, knowing we really needed it. I never thought I would be in that place. Don't get me wrong, my parents would have never let my family starve; it's just that nothing ever seemed to work out for us.

Zack did not like it when I insisted on paying our tithes. He said we couldn't afford to tithe, but I knew we couldn't afford *not* to. I believed that God could get us out of any financial problem at any time He chose to, I just did not understand why He hadn't done so yet. I trusted that it would all work out. After all, God seemed to supply Zack with new work when he needed it.

One day as I drove by a garage sale, I spotted a miniature battery operated Jeep. At age three, Aaron was at the perfect age to play with something like that. This would make his day. Our finances had been tight for so long that we had not been able to buy anything for the kids in quite awhile. I quickly calculated how our finances were doing. I knew Zack had made a couple of sales at the computer store so there actually was a little bit extra.

I pulled over to the curb and got out to ask how much they were asking for the car. The guy said that he had paid over $300 for it, but now his son was older and they didn't need it anymore so he would let it go for $75. When I got home and told Zack about the purchase, he was livid! *How dare I spend that kind of money on this!* I told him we could actually squeeze it into the budget but he angrily told me to take it back. It was so humiliating to be spoken to as if I were a child—with such disrespect and disdain.

As I drove back to the garage sale, I realized Zack would make my life a living, breathing hell if I did not just let this go and do what he said. It was always his way or the highway; there was no give and take, no discussion.

One day my friend Vera came over for a visit. Zack was angry about something to do with the gutters on the roof and was storming around the house. I felt embarrassed by his demeanor. I had mentioned several times to him over the last few weeks that there was a problem that needed to be addressed on one side of the house, but he never made any attempts to fix it until now.

As Vera and I settled in the kitchen with a cup of coffee, Zack stormed through the kitchen saying he needed my help to get on the roof right then. We did not have a ladder so I wasn't sure how I could help him. He wanted me to go into the garage and help him figure it out. I told him that my friend had just arrived and we were about to have coffee.

He stormed off and within minutes I could hear him outside making a lot of noise. When I looked out the back door, I saw him using a garbage can to stand on to climb up on the roof. It looked dangerous to me and I said, "You can't do that, you will break your neck!" He muttered and spouted something I couldn't understand. So I went back into the house and Vera apologized for coming over and said she should leave and we could visit another time.

Vera is one of those amazing, kind people who will stick with you and be your friend no matter what, through thick and thin. At that moment, I looked at her with sad resignation and asked her to stay. She smiled and we continued to talk about our girl stuff, in spite of the drama.

The noise escalated outside and I dared not look. Within five minutes, I heard Zack angrily calling for me. I asked Vera to excuse me again and went to see what was going on. Zack had managed to get himself on the roof, but clearly there was no way down. "Go get a ladder from up the street at the neighbors and get me down!" he barked.

My eyes stared piercingly at him as I put my hands on my hips and pursed my lips. Not only was he continuing to speak to me as if I were his servant, but as I assessed the situation, I saw there was really no way for him to get down. There was no ladder nearby and he couldn't jump so unless I jumped to his demands, he was stuck.

I turned around and went back into the house and explained to Vera that there was no way for Zack to get down off that roof unless I went to get a ladder from the neighbor's house. Vera couldn't help herself and started laughing. It was kind of funny. Vera said she should definitely be leaving and began to get up, still shaking her head and chuckling. I had to laugh too.

There was not much choice, I would have to go and get the ladder and get him off the roof. I could still hear him bellowing in the background. As Vera began to pick up her purse to leave, I suddenly felt so miserable and annoyed that our time was over when she had come all the way across town to see me. *Why was I always in the position of being obligated to a man who treated me with such disdain, contempt and disrespect?* But wait a second. No one was forcing me to do anything. I had choices on how to respond to his treatment of me. It took me all of five seconds to blurt out, "Hang on Vera, don't go."

I marched back outside and looked up at Zack, who now had sweat pouring down the sides of his face. "Are you getting the ladder? How long is this going to take?" he scowled, as he wiped some dirt off his pants. I assessed the situation carefully. He wasn't going anywhere. He had no phone and the neighbors could not hear him because our house was right beside the highway. He was definitely stuck!

There have been very few times in my life when I felt the burn of anger come up from within my gut and out my ears. I could no longer contain the sentences begging to be let out of my mouth. "How many times have I been on the roof of life and you have refused to help me? How many times have I been on the road of life and you made me go wherever you wanted to go, down whatever path you insisted we take?" I was now waving my arms around. He just looked at me as if to say, *Are you getting that ladder yet?*

For the first time in our entire relationship, I held the key, albeit minuscule, to his freedom and there was not a thing he could do about it. I went back into the house and told Vera what I had said. After years of being my friend and walking through many difficult moments together, we began to laugh.

Our laughter was soon hushed as I heard Zack loudly yelling again. I felt another pang of fear go through my being; he was angry.

Then I remembered that I wasn't responsible for his anger. It was not my problem that he railed, demanded, and expected me to run around at his whim. I did not force him to climb on the roof and I was busy with an appointment that had been pre-planned. I went back outside with a renewed determination. I realized that, yes, he would eventually have to be let down, but he didn't have to come down any time soon.

"How does it feel to be stuck on the roof of life? How does it feel to be completely at the mercy of another individual?" For a moment, I thought he was going to react angrily but then he just kind of hunched over and stared at his feet as the anger left his face. It began to rain and he looked up at the sky with an odd resolve. "I have lived this scenario for years with you, Zack! I have been trapped on allegorical roofs; I have lived with no choice but to do it your way and you have laughed in my face."

Zack glanced around the yard as I was speaking and then looked down. I knew he knew there was nothing he could do. Steam actually began to rise off of his back as the rain warmed on his body. That just gave me an even clearer picture of all the steam he had let off for so many years. I looked into his eyes. "Be angry, be very angry. There is not a thing you can do about it and I have lived in this scenario for years!"

I stomped back into the house. I was shaking a little from all my emotions and I knew there was a resolve in my heart to not be pushed around anymore. At least for this one day, on this one occasion, he could not make me do anything. Whether it was right or wrong, I had a sense there would be no retribution on the part of God or Zack towards me for my bold stand. I could see in Zack's face that there was a certain concrete understanding of the irony that had presented itself. There was really no denying that he lived life on his terms and his terms alone. But on this one lone day, he was stuck on the roof of life and there was no way down unless I helped him.

Vera and I sat and talked for about 30 more minutes as it rained outside, making the roof even more dangerous for Zack. He could not move because now it was also slippery. Finally, we knew our visit was over and the quietness was interesting to me. Zack was not even trying to get my attention. *Was he in a coma?*

As Vera drove away, I went to the back of the house to see what was going on. I had never seen that look on his face before. He was a beaten man and he knew it. I knew that feeling well, it's called powerlessness—complete and utter subjection to the will of another. I was not used to being on this side of the fence. I had a certain sense that circumstances had conspired to bring some clarity to all of us.

I trudged up the street and got a ladder, brought it around to the back of the house, and held it as Zack slowly and carefully made his way down. Not another word was spoken the day's events until many months later when he let out a slight snicker about it all. I wish I could say the moral of the story stuck and Zack realized how controlling he was and how powerless I felt in our relationship, but this memory, now comical to both of us, did not bring any lasting change.

I asked myself many times if the difficulties Zack experienced as a young boy led to the troubles we now faced. As stories of his past began to unfold, I found that he quite literally had to be an adult when he was 12 in order to help his parents cope with their own crisis. I started to understand that there were few in life who could survive that kind of upbringing and not be extremely wounded.

One of my favorite preachers, T.D. Jakes said, "Now perhaps you've been around the block a few times and made some mistakes and blown some chances, and the enemy has said to you that you are beyond repair. But God keeps calling you by your name and not your shame. Listen to Him. You must hear God call you by name until you are so filled with '*Whose*' you are that you forget what you have done. He is saying, 'Beloved, I want you, I've already paid the price to buy you back, come home.'"

God does not take back your destiny when you fail. You might not believe in it, you may never choose to walk in it, you may even feel horribly disqualified, but God does not take it back. The enemy will tell you that it's too late. In fact, if he can just get you to believe your own negative thinking, he has won. Romans 11:29 says, "God's gifts and His call are irrevocable. [He never withdraws them when once they are given, and He does not change His mind about those to whom He gives His grace or to whom He sends His call.] "

God fashioned, designed and shaped your journey, building spectacular plans into the very fiber of your being. Your journey is specific to you. Nobody else can do your life the way you can. We all take detours and may even make it tough on God to bring about His purposes through our fallible ways, but if we remember "who" we are and "Whose" we are, our detours will simply lead us right back to the very intersection that leads to our victory.

The schematics may vary a little as God reconfigures our disasters back into miracles, but we will get to live out our purpose no matter what, as long as we put God first, turn from evil, and walk powerfully into the redemption He died to give us. You're the only one who can stop your journey and He's the only One who can take it over the top!

Zack looked after the kids as I went off to a weekend women's conference. I love being in the presence of God and this was a wonderful time with friends and the Word. The Lord knit my heart to the speaker and I had the opportunity to share with her a bit of my journey. I was so blessed by the Word and the power of God at this event; it ministered healing waters over my soul.

The speaker had an encouragement for me at lunch. She came over from her table and knelt down beside me and told me that God would bring about opportunities in the future for me to speak again. She said to keep receiving the healing and let God complete His work in my life.

I remember feeling my heart beating, knowing that this Word was from the Lord. I was so excited that God would see me and breathe hope for a future into my soul. I'd always hoped that I would be able to teach a Bible class, or if that was asking too much, then maybe lead a small home group. Maybe some new converts or overseas students might benefit from that which was hidden in my heart.

I remembered too, that I had received a prophetic word during our early married days, in which a seasoned woman of God said to me, "You will be like the Energizer Bunny; you will keep going and going and going. You are going to laugh and laugh in the days to come at what the Lord is going to do." The only thing I thought at the time was, *I pray He gives me that energy and that laughter because I cannot find it right now on my own.*

This word came to me long before the cross experience, but my deep sadness kept me from having faith this prophecy would ever come to pass so I simply buried it deep inside my being. Soon an opportunity came for me to teach a ladies' Bible study at church and I chose the book by Liz Curtis Higgs, *Bad Girls of the Bible*. I studied the subjects with great intensity. I knew if God ever wrote a new Bible with today's cast of characters on the earth, my story would end up in a book just like Liz's. I poured my heart and soul into preparing for this class. I made up my own handouts with words to fill in, just like I had seen my mom do so many times over the years. I devoured every lesson and learned from each one.

I realized there were those bad girls who never found the true God, but there were also those bad girls who threw themselves at His mercy—like the woman who poured perfume from the alabaster jar all over Jesus' feet and then washed His feet with her tears and wiped them with her hair. I knew that I was a bad girl who was redeemed by Jesus' love.

In Luke 7, you will find the story of this sinful woman who washed Jesus' feet with her tears while He was visiting the home of a Pharisee. Washing feet is mentioned only 13 times in the scriptures and each time it represents an extreme act of humility and service. This woman could have been a prostitute, we don't know, but no matter what, in her own mind she was broken beyond repair. Her shame was so intense that she didn't care if this act seemed pathetic to those around her. The host Pharisee stared at her with disdain as he thought to himself, "If Jesus was really a prophet, He would know what kind of woman this is."

The irony of this story is that it was the broken, sinful woman who truly knew who *Jesus* was. She needed forgiveness and redemption so badly; there was no other remedy for her pain except Jesus. She poured out the most expensive alabaster jar of perfume over His feet, hoping this act of worship would draw out the words she so desperately needed to hear. Luke 7:44-48 says, "Then He (Jesus) turned to the woman and said to Simon, 'Do you see this woman? I entered your house; you gave Me no water for My feet, but she has washed My feet with her tears and wiped them with the hair of her head. You gave Me no kiss, but this woman has not ceased to kiss My feet since the time I came in. You did not anoint My head with oil, but this woman has anointed My feet with fragrant oil. Therefore I say to you, her sins, which are many, are forgiven, for she loved much. But to whom little is forgiven, the same loves little'" (NKJV).

Years ago in my own shattered state, I threw myself at the feet of Jesus. I loved Him incredibly because He had forgiven me of so much. Our wounds, sins and brokenness are actually gifts that bring the ultimate realization of our humanity and desperate need for Jesus. Those of us who walk with a limp cry out for more than our more perfect counterparts, because we know that if Jesus doesn't heal us, we're not going to make it. My humanity led me to trust in His divinity. His forgiveness overcame my failures and I will never stop adoring Him.

The 13-week Bible study came and went and I wondered if that was it. *Was there anything more I could do for God?* A new freedom, joy and peace now filled my heart. But I still had this place deep within my soul that cried out for more and it wouldn't be quenched.

# 7

# THE CALL IS
# NOT REVOKED

*Now when these things begin to happen, look up and lift up your
heads, because your redemption draws near.*

- Luke 21:28, NKJV

L ife had settled into a new normal for me. Managing the daily
emotional challenges of our home became an extreme matter of
prayer. Asking for God's strength was my routine petition. The kids
were growing; my youngest was now four and life beyond diapers was
a good. On an evening in or around May of 1999, a random night at
home was about to change my life. It was the third time God spoke to
my heart so powerfully that it altered the course of the rest of my life.

The kids were all down for the night, the kitchen was cleaned,
and I sat crossed-legged on the family room floor with a big basket of
laundry to fold and a hot cup of herbal tea. Zack was down the hall in
the office on the computer. It was later than I wanted it to be, about
11:30 pm, but time had just gotten away from me that night. As I
flipped through a few channels, I came across a Christian broadcast
I hadn't watched often. A husband and wife team was hosting that
evening and I couldn't recall seeing them before.

As the couple began to chat, I found myself engaged in their dialogue about God and real life. They were light-hearted, yet the presence of God's wisdom was on them as they spoke. Then something happened that I cannot explain—the presence of God entered the room and descended on me. I stared intently at the television as I felt a powerful, yet silent voice, speak to my heart and say, *I want you to do that.* I gazed steadily at the screen. *I want you to tell people about Jesus on TV.*

*What?* My heart began to beat faster. I sensed a heavy presence of the Lord. I had not felt this kind of intensity come over me at any other time in my life. I heard it in my heart again. *I want you to tell people about Jesus on TV.* My breathing quickened as I said to myself, *That's ridiculous; I can't go on TV and tell people about Jesus.* I sat there somewhat confounded and slowly shook my head back and forth. *I'm not a good candidate; I've made too many mistakes. I have no experience; I'm a stay at home mom. I have no training; I wouldn't know how to do it. I've fallen too far to ever be worthy of that kind of call. I'm not the right girl for the job.*

My spirit knew this was a divine encounter. I'm not sure how to explain that I knew it, but when it happens, you just know. My eyes filled with tears as I continued to stare intently at the television. *What is this voice? Who is speaking to me? I'm not capable of doing this.* I could feel my body begin to shake as more tears poured down my face. *God, do You really want me to do this? How on earth would this ever come to be?*

I felt a knowing in my spirit. Without a doubt, this was a call from Almighty God. I melted under the pressure of His hand. The power I felt in the room sealed in my heart that this was indeed for real. *God was calling me.* I was overcome with emotion. There had been times over the years when friends had laughed out loud at something I said and would comment, "Oh Laura-Lynn, you're so funny; you should be on TV." But those were not words I took seriously.

I buried my face into the towel I had just folded and came unglued. It was a very precious moment between my Lord and me. I could not truly fathom that He would use me in this medium to speak to others about Him. I did not feel worthy of this kind of calling. I was not qualified and I certainly had no idea how on earth it could come to pass. I went to sleep that night and didn't even mention to Zack what happened. What would I say? I wasn't sure how I would ever explain it to anyone. It was just the strangest thing that ever happened to me.

The next day I thought about it again. *I want you to tell people about Jesus on TV.* It was just crazy, too ridiculous for words. *Ok God, I will need Your help if this is to ever come about. I don't know where to start.* I thought about all the amateur shows on our local cable access channels. One show featured a guy who looked like Santa Claus with a shiny aura around him from the studio lights. He had a table with a crystal ball on it and he told fortunes. It was quite comical. Surely, if he could get a show, I would find a way.

I quickly got out the phone book and looked up the number to the cable access channel. A woman with a British accent answered and I quickly began to explain. "Well, I would like to do a show…" I excitedly rattled off a concept. "It would be about life, maybe for women, about issues that are important. It would be inspiring and spiritual and…"

The woman quickly cut me off and asked, "What experience do you have in television?" I could practically hear her eyes rolling. "Well … once when we lived in the arctic when I was a kid, we drove past a film crew on the ski-doo…"

This did not seem to impress her but she continued to ask me questions: "What education do you have? Are you enrolled in film school or broadcast journalism?" I retorted, "Umm, no, I'm not enrolled in film school, but in all fairness, I have seen some of the shows you do here locally and the people on those shows don't look like they have a lot of training either." At that, she relented slightly in her tone; I certainly had her there. She suggested that I attend a volunteer orientation meeting. She informed me that the final one for that year was happening on Sunday. I thought, *Wow, that's the same time as church.* I really didn't like to miss church so it really needed to be something worthwhile for me to go. I got all the information and felt good about it in my spirit.

There are moments in life when you know that you are in *exactly* the right place at *exactly* the right time. This was definitely one of them! On Sunday morning, I walked into the reception area and found about 25 other people waiting to be shown where to go. Finally a guy showed up and led us into the studio. As we walked through the doors and could see the set, lights, and cameras, my heart began to beat out of my chest! A joy welled up in my being so intense that I could barely stand it.

I had never been in a studio in my life, yet it felt like I belonged here for some inexplicable reason. They told us to take a seat. As we waited to get started, there were two blonde girls sitting beside me who seemed awfully excited too. "This is fun, right?" I looked at them and they quickly nodded. The meeting began and Ron, one of the directors of the public access channel, explained all the ins and outs of volunteering. I noted that out of the 25 or so people there, a couple of them were actually sleeping. How could someone sleep through such an exciting presentation?

Ron explained that there wouldn't be any positions available for at least three months but he told us to keep calling to see if anything opened up. As he handed out some sheets for us to fill out, the girls beside me said to each other in discouragement, "It's so hard to break in. There's nothing available right now." I smiled, feeling such a peace inside my heart. I knew I was supposed to be here!

The form asked all kinds of questions that I didn't understand. Now I know that ENG means Electronic News Gathering, but at the time, I thought they were asking me if I knew English. I finally wrote in bold letters across the entire sheet, "NO EXPERIENCE." As I left, I walked up to Ron and gave him the biggest smile I could as I handed him the paper. "I have no experience, but I really think I can do this." I held his gaze for a moment and then without any acknowledgement, he turned to the next person to get their paper. I thought, *Oh well, at least I did what I was supposed to.*

Monday morning came and all I could think about was volunteering at the studio. But Ron said it would be at least three months before something opened up. I started to pray, *God if this is You, would You have them call me today? I'm asking You for a sign that this is really what You want me to do.*

Later that day, it was about 2 p.m. and I still had not received a call, so I bowed my head again, *Lord, I know You're busy and there are wars going on in the Middle East, but if you could just move Your hand in this situation and help me get a call today, I would be so grateful. Father, I need a sign so I will know this is truly of You.*

Finally, the phone rang at about 2:30 that afternoon. "Hi, this is Roy. Ron gave me your volunteer form from yesterday and I noticed that you work with computers." Since I occasionally did pick-ups for Zack's computer parts business, I listed his store as an employer on the form I filled out. Roy sounded frustrated and annoyed, "I've had a guy quit this morning unexpectedly and I have to find someone right away to take his place. Do you know how to do graphics?"

I thought, *Graphics! Um, I can't draw to save my life.* I had no idea what graphics were. But unthinkingly I responded, "Yes, I can do that."

"Can you be here by tomorrow morning at 8 a.m.?" Roy asked hurriedly. I told him that I could. After I hung up, I just sat there staring at the phone. What was I thinking? I couldn't be there by 8 a.m. tomorrow morning. I had to get the kids to school; I was a stay at home mom. What would I do with my son? We didn't have money to hire someone. I thought about calling Roy right back and saying I couldn't do it. I sat there thinking it over and realized it didn't make much sense for my life at this time to be running off at 7 a.m. to get to a studio in rush hour traffic for a volunteer position.

I felt paralyzed with anxiety but I couldn't get past what had happened the other night; either that was God or my hormones were way out of whack! I had to admit, it was some kind of crazy coincidence that the station just called to have me show up for work the next day. I needed to have faith. Would I dare to step out and trust God?

This reminds me of the story in Matthew 14 when the disciples were out on a boat. Jesus came down from a place He had been praying and began to walk on the water towards them. Peter saw Him in the distance and thought that He was a ghost. Jesus yelled out, "It's me, don't be afraid." At this point Peter said, "Lord, if it's You, tell me to come to You on the water."

"Come," Jesus said. So Peter got out of the boat, walked on the water, and came toward Jesus. But when he saw the waves, he was afraid and beginning to sink, he cried out, "Lord, save me!" Immediately, Jesus reached out His hand and caught him. "You of little faith," He said, "why did you doubt?"

There could be a miracle taking place right in front of our eyes but fear and doubt can cause us to lose our footing. As I reflect on this time in my life, I realize that God will not ask us to step out of the boat unless He is going to sustain, support and maintain the call He has on our lives. It's up to us to seize the moment, take that step, and know that God is right there with us.

There was a challenge that presented itself over and over in the days and years to come—fear. Fear bore down on my psyche so many times that it became like a well-known enemy that wouldn't stop

stalking me. Fear almost overpowered me numerous times. It stran-
gled, threatened, attacked, ensnared and pursued me ruthlessly.

I spent the evening wondering what 'graphics' entailed. Would I
be designing posters or using a computer to create something out of
nothing? Would I have to draw? But I had an even bigger problem.
I would have to figure out how to get the kids to school and get a
babysitter for my youngest son. I talked to Zack about it and he was
surprisingly amiable and said he would handle getting the kids to
school.

Then I thought of my cousin, Dave and his wife, Chris. They had
been helpful in times past by looking after my kids when needed. The
biggest problem was I really had no money to pay for babysitting.
I called Dave, who has always been more like a brother to me, and
briefly explained the situation. He immediately said that they would
help out for free. It was such a blessing!

Within minutes, all my problems were sorted and I had nothing
impeding me from heading off to the cable station the next morning.
*Well, I guess that's it then!* I was excited, but apprehensive.

Six a.m. arrived and I headed out the door. While driving, I prayed
that God would help me not make a complete fool of myself. I walked
into the reception area and met Anne, the lovely lady who took my
first call. She pointed me down the hallway to Roy, who then took me
to my station in the control room. "Darren is going to train you on
graphics and he'll be here all week with you." *All week,* I thought. *When
did I say I would be here all week?* Then he told me that the graphics he

was talking about was just typing! *Typing!* Couldn't he have just said, "Can you type?"

When I got home that day, I explained to Zack and Dave that I needed to train all week. To my amazement, they both helped out. It was a little miracle of provision. In fact, Dave and Chris helped me for the duration of my volunteering time and never asked for a penny. They were incredible and I was so grateful for them. It was an endowment from God—seeds of provision sewn into my life through their hands.

I loved being at the studio. My shift consisted of working twice a week for the next nine months. I treated it exactly as if it was a job and learned all about how things worked behind the scenes of a live daily show. The director was very cruel to some volunteers if they messed up their jobs, so I lived most days trying to avoid making any mistakes. If someone had the misfortune of making an error, they were publicly scolded.

I worked on a live daily show with a male and female host. I loved to watch the banter back and forth between them. How I wished I were sitting in those seats doing what they were doing. As the months went on, I had a terrible thought, *What if God had really called me to operate the graphics for a TV show with other hosts who told people about God?* That was a very disturbing thought to me. Maybe God called me to be part of the production crew.

I prayed and asked God why I was sitting there week after week doing graphics for someone else's show. *Aren't I supposed to be in the host seat, Lord?* But He didn't answer, so I just kept going. Until God said it was time to move on, I knew I had to simply stay put. I was reminded of the message of Zechariah 4:10, which admonishes us not to despise small beginnings, for the Lord rejoices to see the work begin.

During this time I met some wonderful volunteers—a few of whom had big attitudes, which I later learned is part of the industry. Not one of them was ever from the original group that I had interviewed with. Month after month, I kept showing up and doing my part. Dave and Chris kept helping me out with the kids. Zack even cooperated with everything.

I felt like it was time to see what else there was to do so I went to Roy and gave my two-weeks notice. After leaving his office, I walked down the hall and bumped into a woman who produced local stories. She offered to teach me the ins and outs of producing so I wholeheartedly accepted.

I began to work with other producers who made me carry the heavy lighting kit and cameras. I could see that I was certainly the low man on the totem pole, but I loved every minute of it! I learned how to edit, write, do voice-overs and craft a story. My parents came over to our house one day and I made them sit through the entire role of credits after a program so they could see my name. I celebrated every tiny accomplishment as if it were the best thing that ever happened. Despite this, I still didn't have any opportunities on camera and it didn't seem like there were any in sight.

One day, I got a call from a producer who needed a reporter to run the beat for a parade. It entailed doing an opening welcome and talking to the participants during the parade as they passed by on their floats. Interestingly, I had committed to be in a skit for a women's event that same day at church. We had already had a couple of rehearsals for the skit. I told the producer I had another commitment and asked if he would give me until Monday to figure out if I could assume this task; he agreed to give me until Monday.

What were the odds of me finally getting an opportunity to be on camera and having another fairly significant commitment at church? I loved women's events; it was my passion, and yet, this was huge for me. I went to church that Sunday and went forward for prayer afterwards. I told an elderly lady that I felt God was calling me to do more media work. She prayed a powerful prayer and said, "I feel you are supposed to pursue the media. It is of God." That was all the confirmation I needed from this beautiful woman.

I bowed out of the play and a wonderful replacement was found. Covering the parade was an exhilarating experience. Although I struggled greatly to get out the opening lines from memory, the improvised working of the parade line proved to be my best work. Comments came back that I was a natural and one older fellow who has now passed away said, "Look out world, here she comes."

There were two women commentators for the parade. When I watched the rerun later at home, I noticed that they laughed hysterically at everything I said on camera. It was a glorious day and I was hooked on the medium of television and its ability to communicate fun and laughter. This was where I wanted to be! Who knew?

I began to get little opportunities to be on camera for a couple of local community stories that I worked on with a producer. I spent long hours in the studio to get the stories edited and aired. I was anxious to repeat the incredible feeling of doing the parade, but little did I know that I was not going to be as big a 'natural' as I had hoped.

One day Jim, the producer of the local community news show, had a dilemma. One of his five reporters had gotten ill and it was her turn to host the show. He called me at home on a whim to see if I would be available to host the show the next day. My son was screaming in the background, so it was hard to hear Jim. He said he would send me over a fax of the location and my lines to memorize by the morning. I was ecstatic!

I called everyone I knew to let them know this was it. I was going to be a host for a day; finally I had made it! My girlfriends squealed, my parents were happy, Zack was excited to see me so thrilled, and the kids thought it was going to be fun. This was finally my big break and I wanted everyone to watch it!

I got up the next day and received all the information via fax from Jim. What would I wear? I had this amazing dress I had only worn to church once on Sunday. I picked out some lovely high heels and jewelry to match. Then I put some make-up on. I knew they always had make-up artists to do the hosts' faces, but how different could studio make-up really be? I excitedly straightened my frizzy hair and zipped out the door to get to the shoot.

Since I received the copy of the script so late, I didn't have time to memorize my lines - all five pages of them. *Wow*, I thought, *that's a lot of memorizing!* Memorization was not my forte. I once heard that a woman loses billions of brain cells while carrying a child and giving birth. I had done this three times so there wasn't a lot to spare!

I frantically started reading and repeating my lines as I headed down the highway but the words weren't really sticking in my mind. As I arrived at the location of the shoot, it finally dawned on me that I was covering a fireman's demonstration for kids about putting out fires and staying safe during a fire. My best Sunday dress was a bit of an "over kill" on this cold and cloudy day.

My heart was sinking as my high heels sank into the dirt. My toes now had mud squishing between them inside my nylons. A kind-hearted fireman took one look at me and asked if I was lost. He probably thought I was supposed to be in one of those downtown office towers. I explained that I was waiting for my producer to do a story on the event. He took me into a portable trailer where I could sit down, so I started going over my lines. There were so many of them. *Where's Jim? Was he in an accident or something? Figures that on the day of my big break, the producer would get taken out.*

I frantically searched for Jim again, but he was nowhere to be found. Finally I spotted him and ran to meet him. He seemed aggravated as he said, "You were supposed to meet me at the studio and then we were going to drive down here together." I apologized for the misunderstanding and followed him through the maze of children and smoke.

Jim began getting his camera ready as he explained that we were about an hour and a half behind. The show had to be on air by 6:30 that night, so we would have to do this quickly. He hoisted the camera up onto his shoulder and said "Ok, let's do the first link!" *The first link...? Now which one was that and what did it say?* I quickly rummaged through the pages that were now out of order. "I'm rolling," he said, as I found the first sheet with my lines. I read the first sentence and knew there were about six more after it...but I had no idea what they said.

"Rolling," he repeated. I guess that meant I was supposed to start talking. I had never done this before, but how hard could it be? I didn't get more than 20 seconds into it, when Jim said, "Cut! Ok, try to stick to the script and stay on the topic." *Right, that made sense; just stick to the script. But what was the script?*

I reread my lines and made a second, third, then fourth attempt. Each time Jim seemed a little more incredulous that I just couldn't get it. Finally, he put the camera down on his right hip and ran his left hand through his hair. With his eyes now blazing and the stress of the day wearing across his face, he said, "I HAVE A DEADLINE! YOU HAVE GOT TO GET IT ON THIS NEXT TRY!"

I nodded my head in agreement as I eked out the feeblest attempt, mixed up a couple words, and repeated some dialogue. To my amazement Jim finally said, "Fine!" That was real progress. Then we had to interview a fireman who was going to explain what this event was all about. My mind was going a mile a minute—in all the wrong directions! Jim kept feeding me questions from behind the camera. Finally it was done.

We had three more extremely painful links to shoot, all in record-breaking time of course. By the time we shot the last link, there was actually some sun beginning to poke out from behind a cloud. I kept trying to deliver the lines Jim had written with more of a smile, which he kept reminding me to do. Finally, Jim propped his camera on his hip, put his weight on one leg and wiped his eyes with his thumb and forefinger. He was breathing deeply and paused as he looked up and said very slowly, "Just hold the paper and read exactly what's there."

"Yes," I said as I held the paper and read my lines to the camera. I ended with a big smile, just like he told me to do. "Great!" Jim snapped as he grabbed the tripod and headed straight for his vehicle. Not knowing what else to do, I followed behind him. He loaded his vehicle in silence. I knew this had been a disaster for Jim and definitely for me as well. He looked very serious and said, "You've bitten off more than you could chew today. You need to go to school or maybe read out loud to your kids more so you can pronounce words more clearly." Then he got into his van and drove away.

I walked back to my car feeling humiliated. This was one of the worst days of my life. I wanted to cry, but my mind had gone numb from the trauma. *Dear God, I am terrible on television. I obviously heard You wrong. I'm a disaster. I'm so sorry. I have wasted everyone's time. I will never make it. You must have called the wrong girl for this job. It's a bust.*

As I drove home, adding insult to injury, I remembered that I had insisted on telling everyone about my "big break" and that they could watch me at 6:30 p.m. for my brilliant debut! I wanted to bury my head in the sand and never come out. I would never live this down. I called a couple of people and let them know it didn't go well.

That night I watched the show in horror. There were dirty school kids running around in the background throwing mud at one another. My hair was a poufy cotton swab and it looked like I wasn't even wearing make-up. My mascara had created a "trick-or-treat" effect with big circles around my eyes. The part where I read the entire page was, let's just say … hideous! I was mortified. It was time to give up. I had been given my one shot and had failed miserably.

# 8

# GOD IS READY TO HELP IN TIME OF NEED

*And the king took an oath and said, As the Lord lives, Who has redeemed my soul out of all distress....*

                                                    - 1 Kings 1:29

Over time I came to the conclusion that when life seems too tough to bear, the firing kiln has simply been turned up to high for optimum results. There is a job, a destiny, a call for which you need to be prepared. If you do not go through the fire, you will not be able to hold the magnitude of power that God intends for your life.

Thank Him for the pruning, the process of breaking, the excruciating humility, and the pounding that helps refine your character. Embrace the pain, submit to the course, and press into the learning curve. The day will come when you will reap the rewards from the wisdom you have gained in the darkness. Every corridor you walk, every pain-filled moment, every fear that grips you in the dead of night, every random meeting and inexplicable circumstance, every breathtaking view, every tear and question—He sees it all. He knows your name and will never leave your side.

In Exodus 3, God was meeting with Moses at the burning bush, telling him of the huge plan He had for his life, that he would be instrumental in the deliverance of Israel. This message was more than Moses could comprehend and so he asked God who he should say sent him, what His name was. God replied, "I Am that I Am." When you ask God if He is walking with you during the roughest storm of your life, He says to you, "I Am." When you ask Him if He is going to miraculously provide the rent again, He says, "I Am." When you ask Him if He is able to heal your body, He says "I Am." When you ask Him if He is as crazy about you as He is about that other successful person, He says "I Am that I Am." And He is all that you will ever need.

Every failure, every setback, every painful rejection, every difficult person, every seeming disaster—all of it will be used by God to set a foundation of character and wisdom on which your destiny will be built. Don't let today fool you; tomorrow will yield a harvest that will stagger your mind.

It was hard to get out of bed the day after my on-air debacle. It was as if I had spent over a year of my life heading towards a goal that now seemed completely unattainable. I did not have the time or the money to go to broadcast school. I didn't think my pronunciation was that bad. I had volunteered two days a week for over a year in this field in hopes that God would powerfully open doors of opportunity.

I envisioned that since God had given me that mighty call and had so quickly opened the door to the on-the-job training, somehow everything would fall into place. But here I was: defeated and feeling the same terrible rejection I had worked so hard to overcome. There are days when you run to the Word of God for help, but that day I had to drag myself. I remembered the words of the psalmist David from Psalm 42, "Why, my soul, are you downcast?... Put your hope in God" (NIV).

I sat and pondered what had happened. My main downfall, other than looking unsightly and wearing the wrong outfit for the setting, was that I could not memorize my lines. I used to memorize chapter upon chapter of scripture in high school. What was my problem now? Hebrews 4:16 says, "Let us therefore come boldly to the throne of grace, that we may obtain mercy, and find grace to help in time of need" (NKJV). As pitiful as I sounded that day, there was a relationship I had built with my Heavenly Father that made this kind of authenticity possible. God has very big shoulders and He can take my cries and complaints. It's only when we know Him that we become bold in running to Him with our every concern and disappointment. His throne of grace is always there, waiting for us to come and receive His help and support in desperate times. There is a temptation to run from God when we feel like we have failed in a duty or calling, but He wants us to run towards Him.

Many of us have had earthly parents or authority figures who have deeply scolded us or been angry when we did not perform up to their standard. God loves us no matter how we perform, whether good or bad, Olympic quality or below standard. On that day, I reminded myself that God loves me in spite of my accomplishment or lack of it.

Accepting my humanity was a significant and profound process in my journey to the cross. Some of us are perfectionists while others just like to appear perfect. The problem comes when we encounter numerous situations in life that highlight the truth that we are not, cannot, and will never be perfect. We are failures in and of ourselves.

There is a hidden blessing in personal failure. Over the years I have embraced the gift of truly knowing that I am human. I have become comfortable with my frail humanity, not so I can simply accept it, but so I can accept Christ's identity as a covering for mine. I didn't have the luxury of hiding behind a polished reputation, successful career, or a facade of a life well lived. In truth, it is not a luxury to hide behind any of those things because they leave us in denial of our actual base nature. We hide behind such a façade in an attempt to conceal the truth that we have all sinned and come short of the glory of God.

At this juncture, I knew I was human, fallible, and not anywhere near perfect. Thank God that He uses the foolish to confound the wise. Recognition of my failures put me in the perfect position to take back the territory that had just been stolen from me. As I sat there that morning, I had this amazing, God-inspired idea. What if I bought a tape-recorder and recorded my links and then listened back through a pair of hidden earphones, speaking the lines as I heard them?

That's exactly what I did. I read entire news articles into the recorder and then I repeated the words out loud as I heard them play back in my ear. It was brilliant! I practiced this over and over again. The next day when I was back at the studio shooting and editing a story with another producer, I saw Jim hard at work in his editing bay. Just before I left for home, I gathered up my courage and went over and thanked him for the opportunity he had given me. He gave me a polite smile. Then I proceeded to tell him about the whole recorder concept and how it worked. He didn't look enthralled as he muttered, "Sounds interesting." I knew it would be a cold day in Hawaii before he would willingly use me again to host his show!

I continued to come in two days a week with a producer to shoot a story, do voice-overs, and help edit the piece to air. It was almost embarrassing to keep running into Jim in the hallways. One time before going home, I dropped something off close to his office and overheard him talking on the phone. In a dismayed tone he said, "Well let me know if you get better. This is really late notice and I'm not sure I can find anyone to replace you." After he finished the call, he turned around and looked right at me. "Yea, I don't have a host for tomorrow's show," he leaned back in his chair and put both hands over his face.

"Oh," I said, wishing I could help him but knowing that I was definitely his last choice on earth. He leaned on his elbows over his desk, holding his chin up. Deafening silence permeated the room. As I turned to leave, out of the corner of my eye I saw him slowly glance my way. I paused and looked back at him. With an almost nauseated look of desperation he said very slowly, "Do you want to try it again?"

"Um yes, I think I would be better this time … with my recorder." I felt my heart skip. I went home delirious with joy! The timing of walking into that office, with Jim being totally strapped with no host for the next day's show and having no other choice, was nothing short of a miracle.

I spent the whole evening reading into my recorder then playing the recording back while saying out loud what I heard. I did this looking in the mirror as well, so I could see if I really appeared natural. I input articles on nuclear fusion and on how President Clinton's peace talks at Camp David with leaders from Israel and the Palestinian Authority ended unsuccessfully. In all of this, I looked like I knew exactly what I was talking about. I let out a huge sigh of relief. I went to bed thanking God for this brilliant suggestion He had gently whispered into my ear.

Pursue your purpose with relentless tenacity. Proverbs 18:16 says, "A man's gift makes room for him and brings him before great men" (NKJV). When you begin to step into that place you know God designed just for you, it will be the ride of your life! God will take you to incredible places you never dreamed possible. I think for all of us there is a season where we might not truly know what it is that God wants us to do or what He is up to, but don't be discouraged. Just put one foot in front of the other, walk in obedience to God's Word and follow hard after His heart. Press into knowing who God is and when you seek Him first, all these other things will be added to you.

I love what the Bishop of London, Rev. Richard Charters, said at the wedding of William and Kate. "Be who God meant you to be and you will set the world on fire." As another great preacher, Erma Bombeck once said, "When I stand before God at the end of my life, I would hope that I would not have a single bit of talent left and could say, 'I used everything You gave me.'" May our prayer today be, "Father help me to use everything You've given me, and may it set the world on fire!"

I got out of bed the next morning with a jump. This was the day I could redeem my failure and start on a clean slate. There was no doubt in my mind I would be successful. I wore appropriate attire, caked on the make-up, remembering that it looked as though I hadn't worn any the last go-round, and even met Jim at the right place this time.

Jim was quiet as we drove to the Pacific National Exhibition. I secretly wondered if he was dreading the day. I read over my lines and was going to record them as soon as we arrived on location. I found a quiet spot behind a statue to recite the day's copy into the tape-recorder. I quickly played it back and I was ready to go! Jim set up the shot and I got in position. This was it! It was so exciting!

I rewound the link to the right spot on the tape and fastened the recorder to my belt. I had memorized where the play, stop and rewind buttons were so I could easily maneuver them behind my back. As Jim said "Rolling," I knew exactly what to do. I pressed play and we were off. "Weeeellllcccoommme IIII'mmm Laaauuurrraaa---Lyyyynnnnn..." the recorder sounded like Darth Vader dying. It was replaying at a very slow speed. "Um, it's stuck or something," I said to Jim as I could see panic loom over his face. "Uh, I think it just needs a minute..." I took the device off my belt and hit it a couple of times. Then I listened to it and it worked just fine.

I said, "Ok sorry, I'm ready now," and Jim put the camera back on his shoulder with his eye up to the lens. "Rolling," he said and I pressed play again. "Weeeellllcccoommme IIII'mmm Laaauuurrraaa---Lyyyynnnnn, wweeee aaarrreeee aaaaaatttttt ttttttttthhhhhhheeeeeee…" *Oh my goodness! The recorder was acting up. God in heaven help me! This cannot be happening.*

I grabbed the recorder off my belt and banged it against my leg and then slapped it. I hit rewind and then played it again and it sounded perfect. I listened a little longer this time and within about 10 seconds it went into the slow speaking mode again. *Jesus please help a girl out, Jim is going to kill me. This is my last chance.* I looked closely at the recorder and could see a tiny indicator for battery levels. It was almost dead. Of course it was! I had used it for hours and hours over the last few days to practice for this very moment. Why didn't I think to bring more batteries?

Jim rummaged through his bag and I looked up and down the causeway of the fair grounds to see if someone might be selling batteries. Finally Jim walked straight up to me and handed me the most glorious gift I had ever seen——batteries. As I thanked him, I tried to hide the fact that I was pretty close to hyperventilating and falling into the fetal position. I prayed as I quickly swapped out the batteries. *Dear God, find mercy in Your heart.* The tape played back my voice in a normal tone. *Thank you, Jesus.*

We began again and it still took me two tries to do the link, just to get comfortable with the pacing. I could actually speed up or slow down the read on the recorder. In any case, it all got done in record time——at least as far as I was concerned.

The next link and the following three links were easy. Once in awhile, Jim told me to do a retake because my delivery looked a little awkward. It was a great day. I even got a smile from Jim——a small glimmer of hope that he might give me another shot. He seemed to understand how difficult this had been for me and that somehow the really crazy solution that had presented itself had indeed worked.

That night I bowed my head in gratitude to a wonderful God who knows our shortcomings and weakness and comes to our rescue, time and time again. I knew I was at a disadvantage coming into this. I was older than most people who try to start a career in this industry and I wasn't even doing this to have a career. I knew God had called me and I wasn't the easiest person to train. D.L. Moody said, "Moses spent 40 years thinking he was somebody; 40 years learning he was nobody; and 40 years learning what God can do with a 'nobody.'"

I knew I was a 'nobody.' I had been given the precious gift of failure, brokenness, weakness and inadequacy. Without this gift, I might have thought I was something in and of myself. I had no choice but to let God become the Way, the Truth, and the Life for my poor soul. I clung to verses like 2 Corinthians 12:9 as if they were my very lifeline: "My grace is sufficient for you, for my power is made perfect in weakness. Therefore I will boast all the more gladly about my weaknesses, so that Christ's power may rest on me" (NIV). Could Christ's power truly rest on me?

I adopted an attitude of complete devotion and consecration to Jesus. This become my prayer:

*I am Yours. Do with me what You will, come what may in my life. Though hardship, though suffering, though discouragement and pain will be present, I declare that my soul rests in knowing that I belong to God. He's got my back. I am hemmed in from before and behind and no one can take my joy, my peace, or my stability. I was born to worship and I will do so. God himself seals my destiny and purpose and I choose to rise and not shrink back, to run and not walk, to take my rightful place in creation and not allow any enemy to diminish or steal my purpose. I was engineered to inflict damage on the enemy's territory and I am backed by an army that will not lose. With unabashed courage I eradicate fear from my soul and prepare for victory by the power and in the name of Jesus.*

God made us for a great purpose and we need to live to reach the limits of what is possible in this lifetime. Outside of Him, we will never fulfill what He intended for us to do. We can be at peace in knowing He has given us all the characteristics, talents, and abilities to accomplish our task. However, be aware that without our conscious submission to the Creator, we will miss the most important ingredient to our success—Him. I'm surprised that people try this life without Him when they don't have to.

As I recall my incredible journey, I find myself grateful for brokenness. If I had not been so damaged, I would not have known such healing. If I hadn't lost my reputation, I would not appreciate God's promotion. If I had not seen the darkness in all its ugliness, the beauty and peace of the Light might have gone largely unnoticed and unappreciated.

We are not defined by our failures; we are redeemed from them. Nor are we defined by our talents and successes; our family of origin does not define us. We are defined by our Creator Who calls us priceless—a value that is unchangeable and irrefutable.

It was not long before Jim had other cancellations by his regular talent and he gave me more opportunities to host the show. With each outing, it became easier and easier. I also began to do additional local stories so I could write the copy and get more experience. I loved every bit of it. I never thought this medium would be something I would enjoy so much. There seemed to be forces at work completely outside my control to put me in the right place at the right time.

One day at the studio, I had just finished helping an editor with a story line and was on my way out the door, when I saw a producer for another show in his office. I briefly stopped to see how he was doing. Dave started filling me in on some things he was working on and mentioned one of the shows was looking for someone to pinch-hit for the host when he was busy. Dave asked if I would be interested in this. He had seen me on the original parade shoot, which had gone well. "Sure, give me a call if I can help out," I said as I headed home.

Sometimes these things work out and sometimes they don't, so I just asked God if He would open the door if it was His will and thought nothing more of it. A few days later, Dave called and said the opportunity was wide open if I wanted to host this long-form interview show. *Long-form?* I was just getting used to being on camera for a couple minutes or less. I wasn't sure about being on for more than that.

I met with Mel, the current host, who said he didn't have the necessary amount of time to dedicate to this community interview show and he really appreciated me filling in. *Do they know I've never done this,* I wondered. Mel explained it would be up to me to find my own guests and interview them for a half hour on camera. I told him

I would love to interview some Christian people with amazing stories. He said, "You don't want to get pigeon-holed into that box. People will stereotype you." I quietly pondered his words, but there was a little laughter in my heart because little did he know I was there specifically for the purpose of being "pigeon-holed" into that genre.

The time and date was set for the first show and I asked Pastor Doug Smith to be my first interview. He had been a weatherman for a television station years ago and I thought that would be a neat angle to lead into his personal story of following Jesus. The day of the shoot finally came and from the moment I woke up in the morning, I was sick to my stomach with fear. It was debilitating. I have felt fear many, *many* times. I finally realized that it was just a feeling and meant to be ignored.

I discovered a secret: the first time you do something is the scariest time of all. The second time, the fear is severely reduced and if you persist, the third time is practically a fearless experience. And by the twentieth time, you are able to absolutely enjoy the ride! Basically, the first time almost kills you, but if you just tough it out, you will never face that level of fear again.

Second Timothy 1:7 says, "For God did not give us a spirit of timidity (of cowardice, of craven and cringing and fawning fear), but [He has given us a spirit] of power and of love and of a calm and well-balanced mind and discipline and self-control." I wanted a spirit of power, love, and a calm, well-balanced mind. That sounded really good since I had experienced the other side of that coin for so long.

The children of Israel had to live through the fear of Pharaoh chasing them when they left Egypt. Though he had agreed to let the Israelites go after all the plagues came upon his people, Pharaoh then changed his mind and took pursuit to bring them back to slavery in Egypt. Exodus 14:10-14 (NIV) recalls the fear the Israelites were experiencing and the amazing words that Moses spoke to them.

> *"As Pharaoh approached, the Israelites looked up, and there were the Egyptians, marching after them. They were terrified and cried out to the LORD. They said to Moses, 'They said to Moses,ed, the Israelites looked up, and there were the Egyptians, marching after them. They were terrified and cried out to the for so long. d of a calm and we"Leave us alone; let us serve the Egyptians"? It would have been better for us to serve the Egyptians than to die in the desert!'*
>
> *"Moses answered the people, 'Do not be afraid. Stand firm and you will see the deliverance the LORD will bring you today. The Egyptians you see today you will never see again. The LORD will fight for you; you need only to be still.'"*

It's interesting that the children of Israel had never been so free. They finally had their prayers answered and God had victoriously fought the battle to get them released to enter the Promised Land. It was their time—the end of the captivity they detested. And yet here they were, unable to walk into the joy of it all, because their old enemy was chasing them.

Instead of rising up in faith and saying, "We have seen the hand of God bring ten plagues on our enemies, we know who our God is and we will trust in Him until we have complete victory," they cowered in fear. They even stated that they would rather return to Egypt than die in the desert. But God didn't take them out of bondage to let them die in the desert. They did not know who their God really was. This must have grieved the Father's heart. It still grieves Him today when we let simple, unnecessary, needless fear take the rightful inheritance that He has for us.

I love the final verse of this passage in which Moses tells them that they will never see these enemies again. Sometimes the devil strikes at us when he sees there is a huge victory just around the corner. Even though he has been defeated countless times in our lives, he still makes one more final attempt to intimidate us into relinquishing our victory. Moses declared to them, "The LORD will fight for you; you need only to be still!"

There are moments in our lives when the enemy bears down on our back and trepidation threatens to devour our spirit, but God wants us to rest in Him. Simply be still and know that He is Almighty God and the victory is yours. Satan wants to fool you into thinking you need to head back to where you came from, but that's a lie.

Fear is our enemy. It steals our destiny. It stops us from pursuing the call of God on our lives. It debilitates us for no good reason. It is simply an emotion that should be spoken to with the power of all of heaven behind us. We need to declare that God has not given us the spirit of fear, but of love, peace and a sound mind. My fear was so crippling, I had to take myself by the scruff of the neck and simply step out in spite of my fear.

That afternoon as I drove to the shoot for the long-form program, I felt like throwing up. My stomach was wrapped up in a ball of anxiety. There was a moment when the fear hit me so hard, I thought about how to get out of doing the interview. *Did God really call me to this or was it my imagination? If God did call me, then why am I so scared? Why am I doing this? This is not fun; this is torture! I want to go home!*

I reminded myself of how far I had come—how God sustained me and intervened on my behalf time and time again. I began to confess, "All things work together for good for those who are called according to His purpose" (Romans 8:28). I recalled that Isaiah 32:17 says "The fruit of that righteousness will be peace; its effect will be quietness and confidence forever" (NIV).

As the director and floor director began counting down to the start of the show, my heart beat mercilessly. I thought I was going to be sick. My knees were actually shaking. The floor director seemed completely oblivious to my plight, "We're going in 5, 4, 3, 2…" the 1 was silent as he then pointed his finger at me and I thought, *Well I guess I'm supposed to talk now…* "Hello and welcome to the show. I'm Laura-Lynn and we're so glad you are joining us today."

We were off and running. Pastor Doug told this incredible story of how he had asked God to reveal Himself. He said to the Lord, "If You are real, then a bird will land on me." The next day, a bird flew by and touched his shoulder and then flew away. It was exactly the kind of authentic, powerful story I thought the world needed to hear – a story of God reaching down and touching humanity right where they are, even if it was just so a little boy would believe in Him because of a bird.

When the interview was over, I felt as if I could have done ten more. Line them up! It was exhilarating and I realized that if I had given up during the attack of fear, I never would have known the joy of this moment. When God begins to align the foundations that will one day hold your destiny in place, it's an awe-inspiring experience. Satan begins his attack when he starts to see that God is up to something magnificent in your life. He hates you and will send strategic interferences, hindrances, and disappointments to try to dissuade you. Don't fall for it. Fall into the hands of God and let Him fight your battles for you. Your greatest days are ahead!

Don't let others discourage your dream or call. Think of the story of Joseph. "Now Joseph had a dream, and he told it to his brothers; and they hated him even more" (Genesis 37:5, NKJV). Joseph told his brothers his dream and they sold him into slavery, but eventually he became the one who saved Israel and his brothers from a great famine. God used Joseph's family's hatred to propel him into his destiny.

David's situation was no different. In 1 Samuel 17:28, David's oldest brother burned with anger at him and said, "I know how conceited you are and how wicked your heart is" (NIV). Saul was jealous of David and tried to kill him. But Saul was eventually killed and David became king.

Daniel's colleagues tried to frame him but He remained faithful. Then God shut the mouths of the lions and elevated him to a greater position. Moses was displaced as a child and told he was an Egyptian. God knew his true identity and his background He chose Moses to be the platform to lead the Israelites out of bondage.

You may have to stand alone, but when God is for you, no man can be against you! Pursue the call of God on your life. Put one foot in front of the other and never give up. Let disbelief, fear, and negative lies be put far from you. Acknowledge that you were born to do something that no one else on this planet can do like you. You are one of a kind—you are not in competition with anyone and are not to be compared with any other creation. You are intrinsically valuable. Don't let anyone steal your dream.

We need to be grateful for those who have never believed in us. They actually inspired us to be better. Be grateful for every enemy who conspired against you. They opened the door to your next and greater purpose. Be grateful for those who underestimated God's fingerprint on your life. They are now the ones who stand shocked at your journey. Jeremiah 29:11 declares, "For I know the plans I have for you, declares the LORD, plans to prosper you and not to harm you, plans to give you hope and a future" (NIV).

I recently ran into Stedman Graham, Oprah's boyfriend, at the Chicago airport. I interviewed him several years ago and so I said hello. He was on his way to Montreal to do a seminar on identity - what a great topic! I asked him, right there in the airport, "If we were reduced to nothing but a lung and a brain, no other functioning parts, where would our identity lay?" I think I caught him off-guard. He stared at me for a moment, contemplating that very deep question. This was obviously too deep a query for a three minute discourse on the concourse. Lord knows it took me a lifetime to begin to find the answer to that question. I was late for my plane, so I bid him a fond farewell and off we went.

At the cable company, Jim began to call me regularly to host the show he produced. I was getting better at my delivery of the lines and was also learning simple things like what colors enhanced my skin tone and which kinds of make-up would not make me look so washed out on camera.

Mom and Dad devotedly watched everything I did on air. I'm sure my mom, more than my dad, probably questioned if I really knew what I was doing. I remember finally telling her I felt God had called me to this medium of television. She said hesitantly, "Well, don't give up your typing skills." She wasn't kidding. I could actually hear stress in her voice. Mom had always wanted me to be a teacher or stenographer (whatever that was). This TV thing was way off base for her goals for me.

My friends started saying they had seen me on TV. Even strangers began asking me if I was "that reporter girl from television." It was good to be getting some positive feedback on something I was doing. This was new to me. My life was changing. I began to believe that maybe God could use me now. I felt like my journey was finally getting back on track. He'd redeemed me, set me free from shame. He'd made me a new creation, clothed in His righteousness and created with a destiny to fulfill!

There was a fresh feeling that God was releasing His favor over my life. In fact, a respected man at our church was ushering one day and when we went to leave he said, "I need to tell you something. As you were worshipping, I could see there is an open heaven over your life." Well, I didn't know exactly what that meant, but it really sounded good and it did seem as if God had opened the windows of heaven and was pouring out His blessing.

In early 2000, someone asked me if I had heard about the new faith-based station that was opening up soon in our area. I felt a shiver go down my spine upon hearing those words. I had not heard anything about it. I began to ask around and found out that Willard and Betty Thiessen of the long running TV program, *It's a New Day*, were behind it. They carried a vision for about 25 years to own a network across Canada. They planned to start with one station right in British Columbia. Not only that, but it would be about a 15-minute drive from my house. This was really incredible!

There was something about this news that was like an electric shock to my system. I could not explain it, but it gave me goose bumps. I heard that the Thiessens would be at Missions Fest, a large event in downtown Vancouver set up to showcase Christian work around the globe. They were wonderful people and I had watched their program many times over the years. I made plans to attend. Maybe God had a plan in all of this.

Zack began to be less supportive about my work at the station. He started saying that I was just "throwing our kids," at a moment's notice over to my cousins. He was starting on a very negative trend again. I could sense that his relationship with Tyler was strained. Once again, we were walking on eggshells.

Zack became more and more physically aggressive with Tyler. I spoke to him about it and told him he couldn't shove him or push him.

I always thought you should not be rude to another parent in front of your kids, so I didn't want to fight with Zack over this in front of Tyler.

Zack seemed unfairly hard on Tyler at times and was not willing to listen to me for a second about my thoughts on the matter. He would not regard my requests. Zack still maintained his motto, "I'm the boss, apple sauce!" I cautioned him a couple more times with a lot of emphasis on how serious I was. A mother bear in nature is ready to pounce on anyone or anything that comes near her baby—it's no different with human beings.

Zack had shut down the computer store. He still owed thousands of dollars to his creditors. He found a new job with a good salary. But even with the daily stress of the computer store gone, there was a growing disconnect between us. I didn't think Zack actually noticed it because I wasn't really calling him on his anger or control issues, unless it involved the kids.

Soon it became evident that there was nothing I could say that would help. There was nothing I could do to change him or the situation. If there had been, I would have done it. We were still going to counseling and Zack was railing against my volunteering. He said I was negligent and not taking care of things at home. His accusations were not specific and I could not see where his venom was coming from. I was home almost every night for dinner unless it was a late shoot, which was rare.

Zack said I was not being a good wife according to Biblical standards. He was always ambiguous and it was hard to pinpoint specifics of what he meant. I was very frustrated. I couldn't understand how he could not be happy for the success I was attaining. The counselor asked me, "If God wanted you to give this up to bring peace to your home, would you do it?" I was dumbfounded. *Why would God ask me to give up something He had called me to?* I put the question back to the counselor, saying I wanted peace, but would giving up this newfound joy and purpose bring peace? There had been no peace before, when I didn't have this pursuit in my life.

We attended Zack's office Christmas party in early December. I was seated next to his boss and Zack was in fine form, regaling everyone with his funny stories and charisma. I sat quietly through the evening. When it was time to go at the end of the evening, Zack's boss looked at me with an almost sad, inquisitive expression, "You've got your hands full don't you?"

"Yes I do," I said, my serious tone betraying my plight. That was all that was said, but I knew he knew there was a lot going on behind the scenes and I wondered how he was so aware of it.

December 20, 2000, was another day that changed the course of my life. When I got up to get the kids off to school, I was really sick. I could feel the heat of a fever coming off my face as I held my hand an inch away. I never had that happen before. I told Zack I felt sick and he said he would get the kids to school. I fell back onto my pillow and didn't wake up for at least another couple hours. Then I took some medication and lay back down to rest.

Later that afternoon, a gnawing feeling came over me regarding the safety of my family. It was brutal to live with such strain on a daily basis, not knowing when the next angry outburst from Zack would come. Many times before we separated, Zack would jump back into good behavior for a while, but it never lasted too long. I prayed, *Dear Lord, what is the answer?*

I opened my Bible to read for a while, then I had a long talk with Jesus. I reminded myself of the journey. I reminded myself of His faithfulness to me even when I had not been faithful. I thanked Him for His magnificent forgiveness and love that He had poured over me for many years. I thanked Him for redeeming me by the power of what Jesus had done and for bringing revelation to my heart so strongly that one night at the cross. I thanked Him for showing me how He saw me, clothed in righteousness. I thanked Him for calling me to the media, which still boggled my mind.

I prayed, *I am Yours God, take my life, do with me what You will. I will serve You forever and ever.* I sat there contemplating how the house was like a war zone. Things had transpired that I cannot write about except to say as one judge eventually said, Zack and I are like "oil and water." It was painful to live with the threat of anger and rage but I didn't want to go through another divorce. It was too painful. I didn't want to be a broken girl going through a break-up again. I wanted a good, blessed life.

I cried out to God and again had this very strong feeling our home was not safe. The children were growing up in an angry and threatening environment. *Lord, I'm begging You please, please just give me one more sign this should be over—one more solid sign that we need to separate.* Just then I heard the door open; Tyler was home from school. He came bounding up the stairs, straight for my room. He was usually in a good mood after school but on this day, something was terribly wrong.

He asked "Mom, did you hear what happened this morning?" I shook my head. He proceeded to give me a tearful account of how he had felt very ill that morning too and Zack forcefully, with physical aggression, made him go to school. I do not wish to go into the details any further, as Zack has always denied Tyler's rendition, but on that day, at that moment... *I chose to believe and protect my son.*

It took me about five minutes to hear Tyler's story and to comfort him and remind myself of the prayer I had just prayed. I needed one more sign and this was a glaring, flashing, glowing, red hot sign that it was not acceptable to have this kind of physical, emotional, and mental intimidation every day. It was not Biblical and it was not of God. Proverbs 11:29 says, "He who troubles his own house will inherit the wind, and the fool will be servant to the wise of heart" (NKJV).

Zack had indeed troubled our home and he was about to inherit the wind.

There was a resolve in my heart to make some very strong and courageous choices that would rock my identity again. I was tempted to see this as yet another failure in my life, as if all hell conspired against me. But having done everything I could, I stood quietly with God as my Defender. I could not see the light at the end of this tunnel. The storm raged once again, but I knew God's eye is on the tiny sparrow, so I trusted that He would watch over me. Psalm 72:14 says, "He will redeem their life from oppression and violence; And precious shall be their blood in His sight" (NKJV).

If you are going through a difficult time, there is something to celebrate as a promise from God. To the degree of the pain will be the degree of the healing. To the degree of the sorrow will be the degree of the joy. To the degree of the failure will be the degree of the success. If you endure a very challenging time and wonder how it will all turn out, hang on, because God is working to bring about your greatest victory and vindication. "Make us glad in proportion to the days in which You have afflicted us and to the years in which we have suffered evil" (Psalm 90:15).

During the difficult years, I remember it felt as though it would never end. There seemed no remedy to the disasters—no joy that would compensate for the grief. I experienced terrible consequences, both because of my own failure and because of the actions of others, over which I had no control. There is a bitterness that can come from the challenges we face that leaves a terrible taste in your mouth. Psalm 71:20 says, "Though you have made me see troubles, many and bitter, you will restore my life again; from the depths of the earth you will again bring me up" (NIV). God promises beauty for ashes, the oil of joy for mourning, and a garment of praise for the spirit of heaviness (Isaiah 61:3).

Prayer changes things to the degree that we are willing to have faith for the impossible. I know, because I had to work through such pain and shame that only God could heal and restore my life from the pit. I declared powerful statements of faith, even when I could barely speak the words. The scripture verses I kept repeating gave me strength. I spoke out loud to the enemy who wanted to defeat me. I spoke powerful faith words and demolished fear from my heart in the name of Jesus.

I declared over and over, professing faith in a God who would never leave me or forsake me, no matter what my feelings were telling me. This was true for Job as well. He never cursed God; he trusted God. In the end, Job was vindicated. "After Job had prayed for his friends, the LORD restored his fortunes and gave him twice as much as he had before." (Job 42:10, NIV). This passage goes on to say that the Lord blessed the latter part of Job's life more than the former part.

Isaiah 61:7 says, "Instead of your shame you shall have double honor, And instead of confusion they shall rejoice in their portion. Therefore in their land they shall possess double; Everlasting joy shall be theirs" (NKJV). You'll receive double for your trouble. In fact, I dare say the blessing is exponentially increased for those who will walk humbly before their God and stand sure in His endless redemption. If you never give up, your life will be a magnificent display of His goodness. Be comforted today in knowing you can trust God. He has planned good and not evil for your life. He is strategically preparing an incredible future for you.

I called my girlfriend Lisa, who had been a faithful companion for 14 years since we had worked together at Expo '86 in the heart of downtown Vancouver. I explained to her what had happened and asked if she would help me pack up Zack's things while he was at his regular counseling appointment. I knew he was going to explode when he heard about this, so I called the police in advance and asked if they could be present. They said someone was on their way.

I also called a friend of the family to ask if she would take the kids while I dealt with this situation. She said she couldn't and called Zack and told him what I was doing. I knew that she and Zack had a close connection, but I assumed she would help both of us out at this time. Thankfully, my cousin David was more than willing to take the children and help me out.

Zack showed up blazing through the door. He was livid and the rage poured out of him. He began yelling and walking through the house telling me I was "going to pay for this." Lisa was in the back room listening, out of harm's way. I sat quietly on the couch and did not say a word. I prayed for protection and for the police to show up.

It was interesting that Zack never ran to me and asked, "Why are you doing this? Can we fix this or work it out?" He only paced menacingly, spewing his threats and pronouncing his rage. I was calm, though my heart was racing. I had no tears; I had resolve. The Word says husbands are to love their wives as Christ loved the Church. Never once had Christ spoken to me with rage, insults, threats or intimidation. Never once had my Jesus done anything but love, redeem, forgive and cherish me.

The police arrived. Zack called my dad and he came over right away. It took my dad about two minutes to assess the situation and realize that he would support me 100% and not have his daughter and grandkids in this danger. Ironically, Zack had called my dad to come over for his support, but we all knew Zack would get no support from anyone in my family who had seen the challenges we faced. *It was finished!*

The next day, I called Jim at the studio to ask for some time off for personal reasons. I could not see how I could function on camera with the trauma of what had just happened. Once again, I began to feel that God could not possibly use me to tell people about Jesus on TV. I felt disqualified. But this time I did not have any guilt. I had done all I could do—this detour had cost me almost ten years of my life. The only two consolations were my two incredible children, products of this marriage.

Over the next several months there were many frightening and terrorizing incidents. My father was thrown to the ground several times by Zack. The children also witnessed numerous fits of rage, if not physically violent, definitely threatening and bullying. I feared for my life.

There were many issues that led me to begin a court trial to determine custody, access and guardianship. Several police incidents gave me tremendous insight into the difficulty that police officers experience when dealing with difficult marriage breakups. Zack came into the house uninvited with angry words attempting to take things. When I called the police and they arrived, in no time they would be laughing and joking with Zack in front of the house. By the time Zack had spun his story that I was a crazy person, abandoning the family while pursuing my dreams of 'stardom,' the police were often not very helpful to me.

It became a matter of prayer to survive those days. Even though we had changed the locks, I knew Zack could get into the house when I wasn't there. There were several thousand dollars in our joint account at the bank that Zack took out just before we separated and put in an account to which I didn't have access. I had no money at all until the church intervened and made Zach pay for some expenses.

For a season, my situation seemed very perilous and devastating, but God, being who He is, is never intimidated by any man and will carry out His purposes in spite of anyone's railings. I read the Psalms like they were water to my desperate thirst. I love Psalm 37 in its entirety, but the first seven verses breathed hope into my soul.

*Do not fret because of evildoers,*
*nor be envious of the workers of iniquity.*
*For they shall soon be cut down like the grass,*
*and wither as the green herb.*

*Trust in the Lord, and do good;*
*Dwell in the land, and feed on His faithfulness.*
*Delight yourself also in the Lord,*
*and He shall give you the desires of your heart.*

*Commit your way to the Lord,*
*trust also in Him,*
*and He shall bring it to pass.*
*He shall bring forth your righteousness as the light,*
*and your justice as the noonday.*

*Rest in the Lord, and wait patiently for Him.*

# 9

# UNMERITED FAVOR

*They will be called the Holy People, the Redeemed of the Lord; And you will be called Sought After, the City No Longer Deserted.*

- Isaiah 62:12 NIV

I debated whether or not to go to Missions Fest that year. When I decided to go, a dear friend of mine who was also interested in the media went with me. On the way home, we excitedly talked about what an amazing opportunity the event was and we determined to pray that God would open doors for us to walk through. As time passed and the situation with Zack was ongoing and very trying, I could not see how I would be a good choice for the station to hire.

I missed my work at the cable station so I called Jim again. He said that he would have a hosting spot available in the next couple of days. I readily agreed to do the job for him. After the shoot, I felt like I needed to be honest with him and give him a little insight as to why I had dropped out for a while. I hesitated telling him as I did not want to be seen again as 'that girl with all the problems'.

To my surprise, Jim understood and supported me. He also shared a personal situation in his own family in which he had faced the same things. Then he shared something I had not been aware of. The cable network was going to be swapping assets with another large network and on-air talent was going to be paid, very minimally, but a small compensation would be given. He looked compassionately at me and said, "I'm going to see what I can do to recommend that you become one of the hires." I did not really know how that would all work but I was very grateful for his kindness.

It took a month or so before Jim told me that he made his recommendation and if I wanted to accept it, the job was mine. I would get paid $50 per day, five days a week, to do a story and have it ready for air that evening. My duties included finding the stories, going out with a videographer and producing the story on location, doing two stand-ups, voice-overs, and then creating the edit list for the editor.

He also said I would work with Jim Thompson, known around the office as JT. He would be my videographer and editor for all of the stories. JT was a highly respected, long-time employee who had always been polite to me. I was ecstatic about the new position. Maybe God couldn't use my tarnished life in Christian media, I thought, but perhaps He could use me in a secular field. Maybe that's what He had meant all along. *Whatever You need me to do, I will do it, Lord. Wherever You want me to go, I will go. I am Yours!*

David was a great king of Israel and a man after God's own heart. It is written of him in 1 Kings 15:5, "David did what was right in the eyes of the LORD, and had not turned aside from anything that He commanded him all the days of his life, except in the matter of Uriah the Hittite" (NKJV). Uriah was the husband of Bathsheba, with whom David had an affair and then had her husband killed. Yet God saw that when he was confronted, David was a man deeply grieved by his sin and he cried out in Psalm 51:10-13 NKJV, "Create in me a clean heart, O God, And renew a steadfast spirit within me. Do not cast me away from Your presence, And do not take Your Holy Spirit from me. Restore to me the joy of Your salvation, And uphold me by Your generous Spirit. Then I will teach transgressors Your ways, And sinners shall be converted to You."

David declared he would teach transgressors God's ways and sinners would be converted to Him even after his terrible fall from grace. I am grateful that although God sees everything, He is a merciful and gracious God who understands that we were born in sin and depravity and in need of His relentless redemption. Some of you might feel you have made some monumental errors in your life and have reaped some terrible consequences. You may believe that God, in seeing your sin, may not love you or that He has disqualified you from His purposes and your destiny, but none of this is true! We are forgiven the moment we ask and Christ's righteousness becomes our righteousness. We can never be good enough in and of ourselves. Jesus paid a high price to redeem us from our fallen state so our shame could be completely wiped away. God sees us as pure and holy before Him. "For the eyes of the LORD are on the righteous, and His ears are open to their prayers" (1 Peter 3:12, NKJV).

God sees us in our circumstances today. He sees the difficulties and pain, the tragedy and trials that come against us, and He wants to show Himself strong on behalf of those whose hearts are loyal to Him. Psalm 33:13-19 says, "The Lord looks from heaven, He beholds all the sons of men; from His dwelling place He looks [intently] upon all the inhabitants of the earth—He Who fashions the hearts of them all, Who considers all their doings. No king is saved by the great size and power of his army; a mighty man is not delivered by [his] much strength. A horse is devoid of value for victory; neither does he deliver any by his great power. Behold, the Lord's eye is upon those who fear Him [who revere and worship Him with awe], who wait for Him and hope in His mercy and loving-kindness, to deliver them from death and keep them alive in famine."

It's interesting to me now as I look back and see what God has done from the vantage point of knowing how it all played out. I repeatedly underestimated what God could do in my situation. "Now to Him who is able to do exceedingly abundantly above all that we ask or think, according to the power that works in us…" (Ephesians 3:20 NKJV). I remain in awe at life's turn of events. God loved me in my weakness, never left my side through failure, brought me out on the other side, taught me His truths, and blessed me beyond measure.

I thought that JT was married, but he told me he had never been married and didn't think he ever would be. Relationships were too complicated for him. He liked his quiet life and didn't need it to be messed up with girl problems. He had a very funny sense of humor and a gentle way about him. He had seen many volunteers go through the cable network and said, "They all want to be stars but they don't want to do the hard work it takes. They want an easy road." He didn't have a lot of time for those who were not serious about the business—and he had high expectations of me.

We shot stories for several months. I began to feel the pressure of finding the interviews, which was not easy. The whole process of writing, developing and creating a shot list was really draining. The hours were pretty close to full time, plus I was still doing the long-form interview show once a month at the coffee shop. Some days I couldn't even find stories and twice God had to rescue me. I finally said to JT, "Let's just start driving and I will pray that we find a story."

"Seriously?" he said. This was not his idea of a good time. I had no other choice; none of my leads had called me back. We got in the company vehicle so we would be ready to shoot on a moment's notice, then I prayed for a story. We literally drove down the street and there was a woman crying in her front yard. All of her belongings were thrown onto her lawn; she had been evicted.

This was a great story. Ordinarily when this kind of thing happened, it wasn't that big of a deal. But this was spring cleanup week—the week when the entire city put their rubbish and old furniture out on the street and anyone could come by and take someone's stuff if they wanted to. It was definitely a scavenger's paradise! Since this woman did not have anywhere to take her things during the night, people were taking her furniture and anything of value that she had.

We got huge accolades for this story. There was drama and crying, neighbors were yelling, and the landlord's wife even came down and sheepishly apologized on camera saying they had not known it was spring cleanup week. People actually called the station and donated to this poor woman who had been evicted. It was amazing!

The second time God rescued me by finding a story, I could not find a lead if my life depended on it. It was close to 11 a.m. and I had been working for over two hours to find a story for the day. I told JT that I was going for a drive to pray that God would give me a story. "Seriously?" I heard him mumble again.

I drove about two blocks and a taxicab drove across my path. It was then that I remembered that within the past week and a half, three cab drivers had been stabbed. "Praise the Lord," I shouted, "Cabbies are being stabbed! Yes, yes, yes…that's my story!" I realize it was hardly appropriate for a Christian woman to be celebrating the stabbing of taxi drivers, but this story was such an answer to prayer. I got the phone number off the top of the cab and within minutes, interviews were set up and we found lots of cab drivers who weighed in on the issue. It was yet another celebrated success.

The pressure of this daily grind began to get to me. I broke down one day in the edit bay. I was exhausted. Yes, I enjoyed this type of work, but was this really what God had called me to do—community stories? I had never pursued this line of work for it to simply become a career. I received a call from the Lord and had followed His leading, much like a missionary would feel a call to a foreign land. I was beginning to feel like I didn't belong here anymore.

God's timing is impeccable, even though it may feel at times as if He is running behind schedule. The next day I got a call from Albert Lo, whom I had met at Missions Fest. He asked me if I had gotten his message. I said that I hadn't. "I left a message for you with your husband a few days ago," he said. At that point I thought he must have been confused because Zack had been gone from my house for months.

It wasn't until several years later that Albert fully explained that he had called my house and Zack had indeed answered the phone and spoken fairly curtly to him. Obviously, Zack had been in the house without my knowledge. Albert then called Darryl, a pastor friend with whom I had shot a long-form interview a few months earlier. During the interview process, I shared some of my situation with him. I had no idea Darryl had anything to do with the new Christian broadcast station that was being setup, or that he knew Albert Lo. I just knew Darryl was an excellent communicator and thought he would make a great guest, which he did.

Albert said, "We haven't heard from you and we have been waiting for your demo reel to be sent in." I sheepishly explained that I had been busy with work lately, and then my voice trailed off. How was I to explain that my personal situation was tenuous at best and I might not be the best candidate for a job on a faith-based channel? "We would like you to come for an interview this Thursday at 6:30 p.m. Can you be there and bring a demo reel and resume?"

"Uh, yes I can…"

"Ok, see you there!" Albert gave me the address and it was done. *I had an interview with the new station. Wow!*

I had JT help me compile a smashing good demo of all my best work, which looked even better after he added music and some graphic design elements. There is a reason they say "fix it in editing."

By now, with all the practice I had received, I had some reasonably good clips—but they still needed help.

Thursday night arrived quickly and I headed out the door for my interview. During the entire drive to the station, I contemplated the strangeness of this happening. I thanked God for the opportunity and for giving me an incredible taste of what it would be like to actually be considered for a job like this. I prayed out loud, "Dear Lord, I realize I'm probably not the right girl. I understand that. But I'm so grateful You would bless me with this interview. I do know that if this is Your will, there is nothing that will stop it; I will do what You want me to do. However, I get it that it is near impossible for me to hope for this."

When I arrived for the interview, the executives were nowhere to be found. As I sat there for a few minutes and deliberated if I should just leave, they all suddenly came in. Shane quickly apologized and told me they'd had a very long day. There were three men present: Shane, Albert, and the new station manager, Dean.

After the interview, two weeks and then three weeks passed. I knew the station had obviously chosen someone else. On the fourth week, I got a call from Shane letting me know that they were getting close to making a decision and wondered if I was still available. *Still available?* I was nothing but available.

A week later, as JT and I were packing up the vehicle after a shoot, my cell phone rang. It was Shane again. "We would like to offer you the job of hosting the after-movie show three times a week. It's a bit of a risk we realize, with us being a new startup." My whole journey had been a risk. This was of no consequence to me. It was the first time I would be able to host a show that was about God. As I got off the phone, tears filled my eyes. JT heard the whole conversation and smiled. "Wow, that's great. This is what you really wanted. It's so good." I was at a loss for words. This was a monumental leap forward.

The years that followed were absolutely magnificent. I literally drove to work every day thanking God for His favor, blessing, abundance and inconceivable kindness to use a girl like me for His work. We were known as a "multi-faith" station, so our job was to embrace those from every religion. I was encouraged to use "God" rather than "Jesus" because it was a broader word and would encompass more faith groups. These were the terms under which the license had been granted to the station.

I noticed that since we were a new station, there were not a lot of systems yet in place for the use of the equipment. One day I had a crazy idea to do a show in coffee shops. We interviewed real people and got their stories. I booked a shoot with a cameraman and all the gear. I waited to see if someone would ask me what it was for, but no one did. I went and shot the show at a local coffee shop. Then I booked an editor and we edited the show together. The show turned out great and was much funnier than I thought it would be. We called it *Coffee Shop Girl*.

I sent this off to Shane's office in Winnipeg, Manitoba, and he said he would look at it when he had a chance. About three weeks passed and I hadn't heard a word about the show. Of course, I figured he had seen it and obviously didn't think much of it or didn't feel it fit in with the station mandate. I finally worked up enough courage to ask him for his thoughts on the show and he admitted that he hadn't even watched it.

About two days later, I got a call from Shane and he was laughing out loud. He told me he had started watching the tape in his office at the end of the day and started laughing so loudly that others in the office came over to see what he was laughing at and they laughed along with him. He said, "Okay, do 13 of them! Just like that!" He explained they would feature it as a local show so it would help fulfill their programming requirements.

*Coffee Shop Girl* became a local city favorite that developed into more of a mock reality series about a reporter who was completely inept, yet somehow always managed to pull off the story. I even got fan mail sent to the studio. Many said they actually recorded the show every week. This was shocking to me. People began recognizing me in the streets and calling me Coffee Shop Girl. They didn't know my name but they recognized my face.

Walking in God's favor is the privilege of anyone whose life has been redeemed. If you have been forgiven and saved from your erroneous ways, you are the perfect candidate for the favor of God. In Galatians 3:14, we are actually promised the blessing given to Abraham: "He redeemed us in order that the blessing given to Abraham might come to the Gentiles through Christ Jesus, so that by faith we might receive the promise of the Spirit" (NIV). What was the blessing that God gave Abraham? Genesis 12:2-3 outlines it: "I will make you a great nation; I will bless you and make your name great; And you shall be a blessing. I will bless those who bless you, and I will curse him who curses you; And in you all the families of the earth shall be blessed" (NKJV).

Today, by faith you can know that you are a great nation. The Blood covers your offspring. God will make your name great, not your title, IQ, or talents and abilities, but your name will be known as one who is highly favored by God. You will bless everyone you come in contact with and they will feel better for just having been around you. Those who are good to you will be blessed. God will deal with those who rise in spiteful talk against you and attempt to wound you. All who hire you, befriend you, embrace you, and love you will be highly favored. Your life is covered, sealed, consecrated and providentially ordained for greatness because Abraham was blessed. Now your name, life, and destiny is blessed beyond measure!

I kept making choices to honor God with my tithes and finances. It was difficult to make ends meet at times, but I trusted Him. One Sunday I had just been paid and knew I had far more bills than money. I took out my checkbook and wrote a check for my tithe amount. I knew I could really use that money for the needs of my family, but I also knew God had never let me down so I chose to trust Him.

That next week, another host was unexpectedly and sadly let go so I was promoted to do the afternoon video jockeying for the family sitcoms. With this promotion, I almost doubled my salary and was given a company car and gas allowance. I was too excited for words. I could not stop thanking God for this most incredible turn of events in my life. It was truly staggering.

A new station manager named Jack had come to work for the station and we had become good friends. We had long talks about God and pondered the interesting aspects of redemption. Jack loved my work and said he was my "biggest fan."

I had begun to deal with the extensive debt from my marriage to Zack. My wages were garnisheed for the debts from the computer store that had not been paid. I found this extremely embarrassing and asked Zack to help with this joint debt, but he would have no part of it, nor did he help with any other debts. I eventually paid the entire bill myself. I had to talk to numerous collections people regularly and kept telling them the truth as I worked out payment plans. Within about two years, many creditors had settled with me for much lower payouts and some simply wrote off the debt. I did my best to take their calls and explain what was going on.

JT and I started to hang out here and there and he agreed to come to church with me, but said he would not become a Christian. I said that was fine. He could just see what Christianity was all about. At the outset of our relationship, I told him I would not be having a sexual relationship until I got married, if I ever got married again. He agreed to respect my wishes.

He owned his car outright, had a mortgage on his condo, and maintained a perfect credit rating. We began a very long, slow friendship. I was extremely cautious and did not want to make a mistake. I guarded my heart, as the book of Proverbs cautions us to do (Proverbs 4:23).

I began emceeing many events—both secular and Christian. I was a guest on stage at Women of Faith for about 15 minutes, speaking to an audience of about 8,000. I also welcomed everyone to the Gaither Vocal Band concert in our arena, where about 6,000 people were in attendance. It was exhilarating!

On the night of the Gaither Vocal Band concert, an interesting thing happened. I call it "ironic honor" when God gives you a position of honor where you were once rejected. There was a deacon's wife from the church I had attended who told someone, who told someone else, who told me that she would never attend any function I was part of due to what happened with John and me. When I heard this comment, it truly cut like a knife, although I fully understood why she would say this. I held no bitterness towards her. I know God looks on the heart and He forgives us, but man looks on the outward so when they see us fail so badly, they may not be able to get over it like God does.

As I walked up the steps to the stage set up in the middle of the arena, with the spotlight on me at the Gaither Vocal Band concert, I looked across the platform and there was the deacon's wife sitting with her husband in the front row. I took a deep breath. I knew she didn't like me but I remembered "Whose" I am. I remembered that Jesus loves me in spite of my failures. Romans 8:31 declares, "What then shall we say to these things? If God is for us, who can be against us?" (NKJV).

For a girl who wanted to be liked by everyone, I was still dealing with the fact that I would have to let my identity be found in God alone, as my earthly failings would likely keep some away. I took the stage with the empowerment of a forgiven daughter of the King of kings; I felt His strength and knew this was a moment that only God could have orchestrated. Since that day, the deacon's wife has been very kind to me and we have had a couple of wonderful conversations along the way.

John moved on in his life and we came to a good place of communication concerning Tyler and parenting him together—albeit from different homes. I had never apologized to John's parents for my sin so there was a nagging in my heart to do the right thing, even though many years had passed. I asked John if he could set a meeting up with them, and although he seemed surprised, he said he would. Thankfully they agreed to the meeting and I was able to go and spend a couple hours with them, during which, I asked for their forgiveness. This gave me closure to the pain we had all lived through. Shortly thereafter, John got remarried to a wonderful woman whom he had dated before we ever met.

These incidents and many others helped me to heal, get stronger and continually place my hope in Christ alone. I continued to learn that my weakness is my strength. It is a gift, though I didn't always see it that way. I always thought God would help those who helped themselves, but then I found out this isn't even in the Bible. God helps those who cry out to Him. He comes to the rescue of the broken, hurting, lame and shattered. He raises, to astonishing places, those who know they could not have possibly done it on their own. He resists the proud and arrogant who are convinced they must do it their way—He simply lets them.

God's eyes search for those who may have been given far less by natural standards than others, who know their accomplishment will rely on the infusing power of God and nothing else. He takes great pleasure in showing Himself strong to the simple, humble, needy and powerless. He opens doors that leave mouths open. He arranges strategies that cannot be maneuvered by man's hands. He moves one here and another there, giving opportunities to those who have been cast aside.

When enemies celebrate your loss, God sees it and crafts out your greatest triumph. Psalm 18:35 declares, "You give me your shield of victory, and your right hand sustains me; you stoop down to make me great" (NIV84). When you dare to call out to the Source of all true power, you will find the secret to your most profound and limitless destiny. Your weakness is your strength.

We all get the opportunity to learn many of the same lessons - forgiveness, love, judgment and redemption—the foundational principles of the Gospel of Christ. When we learn them, we learn who God truly is. He is not a God who demands our highest performance. He is not the One who insists we strive; He is much too wise for that. He made us and knows our humanity, fallible souls, and our inability to reach perfection. In knowing this, He crafted the remedy that would bring healing, wholeness and power.

When we understand His redemption, we will find the hidden key to unlocking our greatest purpose. He takes our broken stuff and gives us back a priceless jewel in return. We exchange everything that Satan has dumped on us for a brand new life in Christ. When we release our dreams, hopes, pursuits and future to Him, a boundless outpouring of His providential favor begins. As we take one step at a time with complete trust in Him, He makes our path straight. "In their hearts humans plan their course, but the LORD establishes their steps" (Proverbs 16:9, NIV).

There are a few things that we can absolutely expect in this lifetime. We will find friends and enemies, love and hate, balmy weather and storm filled clouds to test our character. We'll pass through deep waters of adversity and trials by fire as we rise to places of influence we could never have fathomed. There's one more thing we can count on for sure: God will walk every single step with us, no matter what we face. Though life, by its very nature, has both good and evil entwined through its tapestry, the hand of God is there to guide, protect, vindicate and redeem us through every situation that we give to Him.

When accusations come against you from those you once considered friends, when misunderstanding permeates a boardroom meeting that you thought should have gone well, when your children have not taken up the cause you would give your life for, you're left asking, *What did I do wrong?* In all of these things and through the midnight hours when questions beg for answers that may never be found on this side of heaven, God walks beside you.

Isaiah 43:1-2 says, "Now, this is what the LORD says... 'Do not fear, for I have redeemed you; I have summoned you by name; you are mine. When you pass through the waters, I will be with you; and when you pass through the rivers, they will not sweep over you. When you walk through the fire, you will not be burned; the flames will not set you ablaze'" (NIV). If you are facing a difficult and arduous time, you can put your mind to rest about this one thing—God has not abandoned you. He knows your name.

In the raging fiery furnace, Shadrach, Meshach and Abednego experienced their closest proximity to the presence of God. When Daniel was thrown into the lion's den, he knew that the God he had prayed to His whole life would be right there with him in the most dangerous and perilous place. These men found out they did not serve a God who was distant, but rather He was so close they could touch Him during their adversity.

Consider one other thing about the case of Daniel. Daniel's success brought about the attack from his enemies. Daniel 6:3-5 (NIV) tells the story.

*Now Daniel so distinguished himself among the administrators and the satraps by his exceptional qualities that the king planned to set him over the whole kingdom. At this, the administrators and the satraps tried to find grounds for charges against Daniel in his conduct of government affairs, but they were unable to do so. They could find no corruption in him, because he was trustworthy and neither corrupt nor negligent. Finally these men said, "We will never find any basis for charges against this man Daniel unless it has something to do with the law of his God."*

Daniel's enemies schemed and connived at how they might take him down. Eventually they were successful in trapping him and having him thrown in the lion's den. Yet, God used even this travesty to turn the tables on Daniel's enemies. In the end, King Darius decreed that every man was to fear and reverence the God of Daniel, because He had rescued and saved him from the lions. Daniel prospered in the very place his enemies had tried to destroy him.

Zack did not diminish his attacks on me. He wrote the station owners, senior executives, board members, Canadian Radio/Television Telecommunications Commission and many others asking that I be fired. He also attempted to get the charitable status of the station revoked. All of this was really humiliating and I had to apologize on numerous occasions to my bosses and those who had taken a chance on hiring me. It was a real nightmare!

Those men stood in the gap for me and took it on the chin as Zack targeted me and the station. Yet in all of this, it seemed that nothing could destroy the favor I had over my life. I just kept thanking God for protecting me and keeping me exactly where I was supposed to be. One thing I knew for sure—only God had put me there and only God could take me out.

I was at an anti-bullying rally at the mall to shoot some links for the afternoon family shows. I had a self-defense expert lined up as my next guest. Before I knew what was happening, Zack showed up and came up to the table where I was sitting. He announced to everyone that I had abandoned my family and was having an affair. At that time we had been legally divorced for two years. I wondered when this would end.

Doug, the host of the nightly call-in show, thankfully was there and repeatedly told Zack he should leave because this was my place of work. Both of my cameramen had started to roll tape before Zack even approached the table so they caught everything on camera. Zack grabbed my long stem microphone and would not let go of it. My self-defense guest gave him a warning but Zack would not step away. Within moments, a fight broke out and chairs were flying around as Zack was taken to the ground and someone called the police.

Other networks were also there filming so it became a running joke that I had brought my own bully to the anti-bullying rally. My producers asked the other networks not to air the footage. Out of courtesy to another on-air personality, they didn't.

That night I was so upset. Zack had vowed to dog me for the rest of my life and obviously he meant it. I called a lawyer and asked how much it would cost for him to represent me to ask that Zack be given supervised access only rights to visit the children, because I thought Zack's state of mind was not well. He told me it would be at least $15,000 and even then he cautioned a judge would probably never grant my request for supervised access only. I made one more call to a charity organization that helps in desperate cases and left a monotone message with the simple facts of my situation. Whether they helped me or not, either way, I would be prepared for battle.

I spent all of my spare time writing up an affidavit. I had already done many of them. The charity organization called and said they would help me, but only in court. I would have to prepare all my own documents. I thanked them and told them this would work perfectly.

We went to court and in the hallway I tried to negotiate, through our lawyers, a severely reduced access schedule instead of going in to ask for supervised access only. I did this because I wanted to avoid court and I wanted to show mercy to Zack. I was also hoping that this would stop his vicious attacks on me because it was affecting our children. But he would have none of it. He was bent on destroying me. There was no reasoning with him and to my dismay, we both walked into the courtroom to lay our positions before the judge.

Zack testified that I had incited the events at the mall. He claimed that I had attempted to kidnap the children from him and that was why he had approached my set. None of this had any truth to it. After the incident, I called my cousin Velma to come and get the children from the mall so they would not witness their father being questioned by the police.

Zack and his lawyer had not seen the videotape prior to the hearing. My lawyer simply read out, verbatim, my affidavit and then the judge asked to see the video. All parties agreed. When it was over, the judge calmly placed her glasses on her nose and looked over at Zack like a cross schoolteacher and said, "To think you told me that she incited the events of that day!" She shook her head and quickly rendered her verdict.

Zack was given only supervised access to the children until such a time as he could get a counselor to vouch that he had sufficiently dealt with his issues. I knew the kids saw their father cry that day as he said goodbye and it truly broke my heart. I prayed for God to heal this situation in its entirety. Shortly thereafter, a date was set for a ten-day trial to finally divide the assets, debts, and custody and guardianship of the children. This became a 40-day trial spread over two years since we were both representing ourselves. Zack called 22 witnesses and I called five, including myself. It was a long couple of years in more ways than one.

There are times when we will be under direct fire from the enemy. I'm not talking about when we run out of gas, lose our keys, or experience some inconvenience like that; we all have those days. I'm talking about when the enemy who hates us, the devil, roams about like a lion roaring, seeking someone to seize and devour, (1 Peter 5:8). Ephesians 6:13 says, "Therefore put on the full armor of God, so that when the day of evil comes, you may be able to stand your ground, and after you have done everything, to stand" (NIV).

The devil comes against us with what Paul calls "fiery darts" (Ephesians 6:16, NKJV). The Amplified version calls them "flaming missiles of the wicked one." The enemy tells us lies about our situation, plants false insecurities, and tries to hit us where he knows we are vulnerable. John 8:44 says this about him, "When he speaks a falsehood, he speaks what is natural to him, for he is a liar [himself] and the father of lies."

You cannot believe one word that serpent speaks to your heart. He will diminish you and attempt to weaken your faith in the trial you face. He will also tell you that you are not who the Word of God says you are. "We are more than conquerors and gain a surpassing victory through Him Who loved us" (Romans 8:37).

Daniel 7:25 says of our enemy that, "he shall speak words against the Most High [God] and shall wear out the saints of the Most High." The enemy wants to steal your rest and wear you out. The Word clearly tells you how to combat that attack in Isaiah 40:31: "Those who hope in the LORD will renew their strength. They will soar on wings like eagles; they will run and not grow weary, they will walk and not be faint." These were desperate times in my life and I hung onto every word in Scripture to get me through.

There are familiar spirits who know you very well and will craft a snare or trial for your soul to keep you from walking in victory and attaining all that God intends for your life. In his book *The Three Battlegrounds,* Francis Frangipane said, "Satan will not continue to assault you if the circumstances he designed to destroy you are now working to perfect you."[1] If we demolish the lies of the enemy and speak only the truth, the devil will just get frustrated trying to defeat us. He will see that what he meant for evil is now working for good. As you submit to God, the enemy will leave you alone.

Although this time in my life gave me great cause for distress, I was undergirded with a supernatural strength that got me through. Psalm 91:1 declares, "He who dwells in the secret place of the Most High shall abide under the shadow of the Almighty. I will say of the LORD, 'He is my refuge and my fortress; My God, in Him I will trust.' Surely He shall deliver you from the snare of the fowler" (NKJV).

---

[1] Francis Frangipane, *The Three Battlegrounds: An In-Depth View of the Three Arenas of Spiritual Warfare: The Mind, the Church and the Heavenly Places* (Cedar Rapids: Arrow Publications, 2006). 34-37.

# 10

# LOVE COVERS
# A MULTITUDE OF SINS

*And coming in that instant she gave thanks to the Lord, And spoke
of Him to all those who looked for redemption in Jerusalem.*

- Luke 2:38

JT and I had been good friends for three and half years. He had been
faithful to go to church and found the God who loves us incredibly.
His mother was so thrilled that her quiet boy was potentially going to
be in a larger extended family. I wrestled with the fear that God would
not want me to remarry. I had already made two huge mistakes. *How
many chances does a girl get?* Perhaps it was my lot to be alone.

I love the story of the Samaritan woman at the well who had been
married five times. Obviously she made me feel better about myself.
She was well known to the town for having lived a wayward life. The
Samaritans were looked down upon by the Jews and normally a Jewish
man like Jesus would never engage in a conversation with a Samaritan,
especially a woman. Already there were three strikes against her: her
terrible reputation, she was a Samaritan, and she was a woman.

John 4 tells the story of Jesus meeting the Samaritan woman and
asking for a cup of water. In verses 9-10 we read, "'You are a Jew and I

am a Samaritan woman. How can you ask me for a drink?' (For Jews do not associate with Samaritans.) Jesus answered her, 'If you knew the gift of God and who it is that asks you for a drink, you would have asked him and he would have given you living water'" (NIV). I read this story with such interest because I, too, felt like an outcast and a fallen, discarded woman. What amazed me was Jesus actually gave this Samaritan woman the time of day. In knowing who she really was, He could have simply looked the other way. Yet He engaged her in conversation and offered her something that would change her life forever. She didn't talk to Him first; He approached her.

The Samaritan woman said she wanted this water Jesus mentioned that she might never thirst again. In John 4:16–18 NIV, He told her, "'Go, call your husband and come back.' 'I have no husband,' she replied. Jesus said to her, 'You are right when you say you have no husband. The fact is, you have had five husbands, and the man you now have is not your husband. What you have just said is quite true.'" He was not surprised one bit by her history, present position or plight. As a woman who had been through two broken marriages, I clung to the knowledge that Christ would regard me in my human estate, acknowledge me, and even speak to me.

In John 4:25-26 the woman said, "'I know that Messiah…is coming. When he comes, he will explain everything to us.' Then Jesus declared, 'I, the one speaking to you—I am he'" (NIV). Again, these words powerfully impacted me. At this time, Jesus had not chosen to reveal His true identity to many Why would He choose such a broken, marginalized woman to make Himself known as the true Messiah? I couldn't help but ask the Lord if He would please choose me, with all my failings in life, having not lived up to the purposes for which I was created. *Please choose me,* I prayed. I'm not sure that anyone can understand the magnitude of this hope, unless they have been debilitated by the journey also. *He or she who is forgiven much, loves much.* My brokenness was my gift.

The story in John 4 continues as Jesus' disciples returned and were surprised to find Him speaking to the Samaritan woman. Christians can be the most surprised when God reveals His kindness, glory and power through an encounter with the least of these. Somehow the idea that God would not just use the whole, perfect and successful person leaves us wondering what He is thinking. The Bible says He came for the sick and those who need healing so they would be made well and become vessels of honor for Him.

Verses 28-30 say, "Then, leaving her water jar, the woman went back to the town and said to the people, 'Come, see a man who told me everything I ever did. Could this be the Messiah?'" (NIV). Many of the Samaritans from that town believed in Jesus because of the woman's testimony. This Samaritan woman of ill repute, marred by a life of disobedience, waywardness and shame, became the very one through whom others made their way to Jesus. For a wrecked 21st century girl like me, this was a crazy beautiful thought! I could not help buy cry out the following prayer.

*Dear God, I am that woman who is cast aside. I know You know who I am; all that I have ever done. Thank You for healing my heart. Thank You for breaking me so intensely that I found out who You really are so I would know who I really am. Thank You that no demonic accusation has stood, nor will stand against me as You have barred the assault by residing as a shield in my defense.*

*Thank You that You have used even my enemies to advance my call. I praise You for seeing me in my brokenness and not despising me, but rather loving me unendingly, restoring me compassionately, redeeming me supernaturally by the profundity of the cross and revealing to me Your devotion, Your dedication, Your loyalty, Your commitment and Your consecration to what You began in my mother's womb. Formed in darkness, You knew I would be a mess one day and would need that price Your precious and only Son paid.*

*Seeing the unstoppable demise of my sin nature, even before time began, You created and crafted a formidable plan to fashion a cure that would save me, protect me from myself and lead me to my purpose. I submit my will, surrender my pride, and relinquish my rights to You; I concede all personal gains and yield all control to Jesus! I am Yours alone, created to bow, serve and worship the King of kings. I love You and I know who You are, my life is not my own. I surrender.*

Every one of us is given a promise that God, seeing us in our plight, will not leave us there, but has provided a way to escape the pain and shame. Redemption is our free gift, yet the price was unfathomable. We cannot earn such redemption nor afford the cost to purchase it. But upon our acceptance by faith, it will revolutionize our existence.

I cannot and will not use scripture to justify marital break-up. However, I've come to the realization, as I speak across the country and have chosen to be open about my life, that there are many painful stories in the homes of North America. Therefore, I use scripture to highlight the love of our Father for all of us broken, imperfect people who cannot live up to the righteous and holy standard that God requires. Since the fall of Adam and Eve, no man or woman has ever been able to meet that standard.

I believe most people understand that divorce brings absolute devastation to a life. Families are usually financially ruined and emotionally shattered. The reputations of those involved are marred and they feel unworthy of God's love, disqualified from their destiny, unhappy and unsuccessful. Divorce is one of the most difficult trials a person could ever go through.

Christ told us to love one another, to prefer one another, to be kind, gentle, long-suffering, not angry, and to live at peace and have compassion for each other, especially towards the one to whom we are married. In some homes, however, abuse is an ever-present reality. Sadly today, there are some churches that want a marriage to stay together at all cost, even when there is abuse. The perpetrator may appear to be sorry or even ask for forgiveness, but they have not repented of – turned from – their abusive ways.

I had several difficult conversations with church leaders when Zack asked them to intervene after he had been removed from the home. Zack became emotional and won their sympathies with his tears. Their goal was to reunite us. In a meeting with four men, including Zack, one pastor said if I was not willing to reconcile with Zack, then they would be unwilling to help me.

I softly told this pastor I had not asked for their help. It was Zack who wanted the religious establishment to ensure I would return to the relationship. Though he gave little credence or worship to God, he quickly wanted to use Christ's body of believers as a means to his own selfish ends. At the time, thankfully, another pastor graciously and quickly stepped in to counter this previous comment saying they would indeed help me, no matter the outcome.

When I told them it was not safe for me or my children to be with Zack, one of the men commented that I was using the "safety card." I held my peace and stood strong in the moment. I was shocked by the lack of backing, given the facts of what had been happening. These men knew far more than what I have chosen to write in this book.

In the days that Jesus walked the earth, His strongest words of dissent were always reserved for the religious leaders of the day. They were angry when he healed someone on the Sabbath—this was against the *rules*. Jesus broke the legalistic rules to bring freedom to men's hearts so they could follow Him and enter a deep and profound relationship with Him.

Pastor Culley once said, "Legalism, on the surface, sounds reasonable. Multitudes of churches and ministries engage in the practice. Up front, it looks like a righteous, conscientious effort of the spiritual leaders to keep sin out of the hands of prospective sinners...If the legalists were right, Jesus wasted His time...Instead something compelled Him to go to the cross. Let Him be Lord of your life! HE is the living rulebook! You'll not go wrong following Him."

Ezekiel 36:27 (NIV) says, "And I will put my Spirit in you and move you to follow My decrees...." Even though this verse is from the Old Testament and was written long before Jesus came to restore relationship, it captures the essence of the heart of God. A friend of mine named Julie, wrote a profound thought based on this verse: "It's not about what God wants or needs ME to do for HIM. It's about what HE wants to do in, through and for ME. He offers abundant life, not bondage." God will move you to follow His decrees because you love Him.

God's principles are there for our protection and I believe in those standards. However, as one pastor recently said, the church has made divorce the unforgiveable sin. When women actually have to ask in today's church if they have to stay with an abusive man or if they have permission to separate and possibly divorce from a man who is physically, spiritually or mentally abusive, something is wrong.

I recently attended a symposium at ACTS Seminaries at Trinity Western University. There was a profound moment in one of the sessions when a non-Christian former lawyer who now advocates for abused women said, "I am supporting the women that you have not supported in the church. The laws of our land are based on Judeo-Christian values, which are not my foundational belief system; they are your belief system. They support the protection of the abused and hurting. Yet, the church has not stood with women in their own congregations who have needed security." There was a hushed gasp of clarity as pastors and ministers from many denominations realized a tragedy has taken place under our church roofs.

Colossians 2:14 speaks to the issue of obeying the letter of the law to the point that it mitigates the true spirit of relationship with God, relationship that has been made possible through Christ's work on the cross: "Having cancelled and blotted out and wiped away the handwriting of the note (bond) with its legal decrees and demands, which was in force and stood against us (hostile to us). This [note with its regulations, decrees, and demands] He set aside and cleared completely out of our way by nailing it to [His] cross."

Rules were created by a holy God to show us that we could not possibly live up to them. They reveal the reality that we need a Savior to rescue us from our sinful ways. Jesus nailed the law, rules and the note with its regulations, decrees and demands to the cross. Legalists maintain rules even at the expense of people. The Pharisees were angry with Jesus for healing on the Sabbath, rather than rejoicing that a sick man was now free.

There has been a wrongful stand by the church to keep marriages together when the security of women and children are at stake. In an attempt to observe the regulation concerning divorce, individuals have been robbed of the freedom, safety, and power that is theirs in Christ. God will not martyr His precious children's emotional, physical and spiritual well being on the altar of a rule.

Luke 4:16-20 tells of the time when Jesus spoke in His hometown of Nazareth at the synagogue. He repeated words written long before in the book of Isaiah – words that prompted some of those who heard to try to kill Him: "The Spirit of the LORD is upon Me, because He has anointed Me to preach the gospel to the poor; He has sent Me to heal the brokenhearted, to proclaim liberty to the captives and recovery of sight to the blind, to set at liberty those who are oppressed; to proclaim the acceptable year of the LORD" (NIV).

Dr. Nancy Nason-Clark is a Professor of Sociology at the University of New Brunswick in Canada. She is the author of numerous books, which I recommend, including *The Battered Wife: How Christians Confront Family Violence, No Place for Abuse,* and *Refuge from Abuse.* She is also co-editor of *Woman Abuse: Partnering for Change.* She is the Director for the RAVE Project (Religion And Violence E-learning). She spoke at the symposium I attended and gave the most powerful message I have ever heard given to the church today on the subject of domestic abuse. These comments were taken from a feature she wrote entitled, "Holy Hush or Shattered Silence: Abuse and the Christian Church."[2]

Most clergy have never preached a message that explicitly condemns wife abuse, child abuse or violence in the home. *There is a holy hush.*

Most ministers do not include any information about violence in their premarital counseling package with couples. *Holy Hush.*

Most leaders of youth groups never talk about violence in dating relationships nor do they encourage young men and

[2] Nancy Nason-Clark. "Holy Hush or Shattered Silence: Abuse and the Christian Church." *New Wineskins,* January-February 2008. http://www.wineskins.org/filter.asp?SID=2&co_key=1499

women to identify and practice healthy interpersonal encounters. *Holy Hush.*

When women who have been victimized come to their faith communities for help, ministers and other religious leaders are often reluctant to refer them to outside community resources—to the experts. *Keep it hushed.*

Sometimes, religious leaders do not offer spiritual comfort to victims—like reading passages from the Bible condemning violence. *Hush. Hush.*

Yet, there is a rumbling in some congregational closets that cannot be silenced. It occurs when you least expect it. It is getting louder all the time. It is determined to shatter the silence about abuse, particularly in families of faith. People of faith, shatter the silence! Bring hope to those who feel their hope has been extinguished.

When clergy counsel a woman who has been battered to consider safety her top priority, the silence is *shattered.*

Jesus shattered the rules when He saved an adulterous woman from being stoned, which was the foreknown, deserved judgment in the Old Testament for such a sin. Jesus defied the rules and rocked the policies and procedures of the religious establishment of the day when He healed a man on the Sabbath. Jesus broke the rules to talk to a Samaritan woman of ill repute. And Jesus still stands in between you and those who throw stones of judgment.

In Psalm 66:9-12, David cries out, "He has preserved our lives and kept our feet from slipping. For you, God, tested us; you refined us like silver. You brought us into prison and laid burdens on our backs. You let people ride over our heads; we went through fire and water, but you brought us to a place of abundance." There will be times when we do not understand why we are facing a terrifying circumstance. It may even seem as though God does not see what is happening. We may experience loss or our hopes might be crushed. David spoke of silver, which is refined in the fire of adversity. Every hardship you face will work to purify the precious gift that resides within you. The most amazing secret is that it will eventually all work together for good to bring about God's will and destiny for your life.

Jack and a new producer, Don, called me to the boardroom. They were excited to talk to me about the possibility of doing a more serious news-style show. I was a little surprised because in truth, I had never desired to be a hard news person. My dad was a true news junkie and I loved to hear what he thought about the elections or wars and what it all meant to us, but I actually found it very difficult to follow all the political and partisan viewpoints from around the globe.

Even though I knew in my heart that serious news was not my forte, I decided to give it a try. Jack felt we needed to get *Coffee Shop Girl* off the air after 28 episodes, in order to rebrand me as a more serious anchor type. From my perspective, these were my bosses so if this was the route they wanted to go, then I would go along for the ride, knowing that God would direct my steps. Within a short period of time, it was evident that this idea would not work. When Jack asked me what was west of the West Bank, I said, "The bank?"

Don told me that they were letting the host of the nightly live show go and another host would be hired for a new national show in which I would do the entertainment segments. This would involve interviewing celebrities and people of notoriety. This idea sounded a lot better than the serious stuff I thought I would have to do—it seemed like a good fit.

I married JT, the man I loved and cherished. I loved my work at the station; it was more than I imagined it could be. I was given the opportunity to interview Dog the Bounty Hunter while in Hawaii. Life couldn't be better! But there was still one small issue I had to face—the ten-day trial that began in August of 2005. God gave me tremendous strength to prepare and show up in court.

I became used to speaking in situations that would make many people nervous, such as being in front of the cameras, interviewing famous celebrities, and speaking to large crowds. However, none of that seemed to prepare me for the terrifying feat of standing before one lone judge. Justice Brine was a fair and kind man. I found him to be longsuffering as both Zack and I struggled to follow correct procedure as we represented ourselves. I had spent many hours typing up my affidavit and preparing four-inch binders with over one hundred exhibits and submissions. We were there to divide debts and assets, while addressing custody, access and guardianship.

By the end of the ten allotted days of trial we were not finished, so ten more days were set for several months later. This was extremely disheartening because I would have to take time off from work for the remainder of the trial. I knew it would all work though. I thought the litigation between Zack and me was the biggest hurdle in my life that year when it began, but time would surprisingly reveal that the most difficult trial was yet to commence. It would shake me to the core of my being in a far greater way than the courtroom drama that was unfolding before my eyes.

I've heard that when you are out sailing, it can be a beautiful balmy day, but a sudden change of the wind can cause storm clouds to roll in and catch you unaware. Perhaps that's how the disciples felt when they were in a boat and a furious storm began to brew. They were terrified—yet Jesus was asleep in the bottom of the boat. Matthew 8 tells the story of how the disciples went and woke Him saying, "Lord, save us! We're going to drown!' Jesus replied, 'You of little faith, why are you so afraid?' He got up and rebuked the winds and the waves and it was completely calm. The men were amazed and asked, 'What kind of man is this? Even the winds and the waves obey him!'" (Matthew 8:25-27 NIV).

It's interesting that Jesus actually told them they had little faith and asked them why they were so afraid. I mean, wasn't it obvious? These men were fishermen and they had spent their whole lives on these waters and seen many storms, yet this one caused them to panic.

You see, Jesus knew who He was and the power He carried. This storm didn't scare Him. But to the disciples, the storm revealed their unbelief because if they had truly known who Jesus was, they would not have awakened Him in that manner. They would not have spoken those desperate words of terror, "We're going to drown." Their dread and anxiety exposed their core disbelief and Jesus knew they didn't trust Him. They didn't know Him and they did not believe that He was who He said He was: the Healer, Deliverer and Savior.

If they had understood the magnitude of the authority and power this Man carried, their reaction would have been completely different. They would have known that the very presence of Jesus bore the weight and influence of all of heaven's supremacy. They could have gently woken up Jesus saying, "There's a bit of a gale outside, but don't get up, just say the word and calm this raging storm."

You might be in that place today—with a tornado of circumstances bearing down on your life. You may wonder where God is and it might seem as if He's asleep and not paying attention to your anguish. The question you must ask yourself is, do you know who Jesus is? Though we do not always understand His timing, His power is undeniable. His plans are profound and can be trusted. His strategies defy human comprehension and God's promise is that He will never leave us or forsake us.

There is no wisdom that can form against Him, no arrogance that will outwit Him. He is magnificent in beauty and renowned for His excellence. He is your all in all—the only One who will make you great. He's your backup in the heat of the fray and the author of everything magnificent you will ever do. Your storm is not a sign that He is unaware; it's an opportunity for you to show Him that you know who He is and you trust Him. It is also an opportunity for Him to see what resides deep within your heart.

I wish I could say I passed through this next storm with flying colors, but it was one of the most jarring tests of my life—it rocked my world. I thought I had dealt with the issue of my identity many times over. *What more did I need to learn?* In hindsight, I now realize that God had shown me that I was redeemed, bought back from Satan's curse by the power of the cross. He then showed me that I had an irrefutable position in His Kingdom as a daughter of the King of kings; I was royalty and nothing would change that. Yet, there was one more place God would need to fortify the foundation of my identity, by breaking any reliance on position, status or possessions.

The station owners I had loved so much were in financial crisis and made the very difficult decision to sell the broadcast license to another large media enterprise. There was a company-wide gathering scheduled to meet the new owners as the Thiessens would be turning the station over to them with their blessing. We knew this had been a difficult choice for them to make. The new executives finally arrived, along with our current owners, and began filing in one at a time. It was an ominous and profound moment and there were circumstances at play that I could not possibly understand.

One of the salespeople from the station leaned in close to my ear and said, "This is going to be so good for your career." I should have been happy but an odd sensation swept over me; a worrying impression that something didn't feel quite right. Perhaps it was the stress and strain I could see on the Thiessen's faces, or as God does so often, perhaps it was the start of His preparing me for the difficulty that lay ahead.

The new boss told us He was of the Baha'i faith. As I look back, it is almost as if this meeting marked the changing of the winds.

Nothing would ever be the same again. We no longer had weekly devotions and the spirit around the studio changed. I woke up one morning with a fever and an ache going through my entire body. Every joint felt swollen and I realized that I had been feeling this way more and more lately. My head pounded and I literally had to drag myself into the shower. My interview that day was with a well-known chef in Vancouver. I contemplated calling it off but I had a producer and two cameramen waiting on me.

I drove and drove, not realizing how far it was to my destination. Then I got lost. By the time I finally arrived at the shoot, I was over half an hour late and felt like a truck hit me. It was an extremely difficult day. About nine months later, I was diagnosed with a disease that explained many of the issues I was having but at the time, I was just left wondering what was wrong with me.

Don, the senior producer, met with me later and had a talk with me about being late. I assured him it wouldn't happen again. As the subtle winds of God's favor began shifting, it seemed as if nothing I did was right in Don's eyes. One evening, there was a political show being taped that I had nothing to do with. As I finished up my work, I heard that a certain candidate whom I highly admired was in the building. I made my way to the lobby where several of the candidates were gathered and said hello and expressed how much I appreciated the good he had done for Canada and then went back to my desk.

Don came over with steam pouring from his ears and eyes blazing, demanding I never do that again because it made it look like the station was biased. What he said made perfect sense. I realized then that I should have paid my respects more privately and apologized. However, it was Don's venom and extreme anger that was really shocking. He had a mean streak and this kind of nastiness had never been part of the station before. At this point, I knew his reaction was personal towards me. There was an extreme lack of grace. Considering his background and the faith we shared, I was taken aback by it.

On another day, we were going to interview Bob from *Sesame Street*. I remembered watching him when I was a little kid and looked forward to meeting him. I had some voice-overs to finish writing at the studio for some other interviews we had already completed and I knew if I got them done, I would not have to return later that evening, which meant I could get home to my family. I quickly finished them with plenty of time to get to the interview.

On the way, the assistant producer and I got stuck in road construction. Traffic was at a complete standstill. I already knew Don seemed to have it out for me so I distinctly remember thinking, *With the way things are going, I just know I am going to get blamed for this.* Sure enough, we were late getting to the shoot, and indeed Don was more than angry that we hadn't left earlier.

He looked at me furiously and wanted to know if I had left later because I was trying to avoid coming back that evening. I eyed him cautiously not knowing how to answer, because while it was true, we did leave later so I could finish work I needed to do and not have to return, I also knew we left in plenty of time to have arrived in reasonable fashion, barring the unforeseen construction. It was as if there was no way to win. The only redeeming factor was meeting Bob, who was even more delightful in person than he was on *Sesame Street.*

The situation at work made me feel as if I was standing in quicksand and couldn't get out. The more I struggled, the more I sank. When I found out I would be doing a regular half hour, stand-alone show for the Biography Channel Canada, all I could say was, "Oh, that's good." I was happy I had this opportunity but I felt so beat up that I couldn't enjoy it. With the opportunities that came my way, I soon had completed over 90 celebrity interviews.

As time went on, however, I knew there had been a monumental shift in the spiritual realm at the station. Since taking on this job five years earlier, everything I touched had worked; there had been favor on all sides—five years of it. Now, it felt everything was slipping away and I couldn't hold on to it. What was wrong? I began asking God repeatedly to help me and to bring back His favor over my life. I had bad dreams about being fired. I started to hate going to work; it literally made me feel sick.

On January 22, 2006, I wrote in my diary, *I think I might be getting fired this week…I got a disheartening letter from Jack, which would have been more painful rather than shocking, if I had believed one word of it. Funny, he's been my mentor and coach, highly regarded in my life and now I feel puzzled by his words. I've never worked harder nor been more knowledgeable about my profession than this last few months. … but now I think I'm getting fired. I've learned a lot as the 'weirdness' has grown. I've learned I must have more faith than fear. I must trust and not doubt God's divine providence. I must rest and let things take their course, rather than try to make things happen. I must focus my attention on worshiping, rather than worrying ... I feel like God is preparing me to accept whatever plan He has.*

I got up the next day and thought, *I have a dear friend in this company and he is the top person here——Jack.* Jack had been promoted by the new organization and moved to a new office so I rarely saw him anymore. Still, surely I could talk to him about the way Don was treating me and see if there could be some intervention. I asked God to turn the tide. That day as I walked down the hall, conveniently Jack was right there. I was about to ask him if we could please meet to discuss my concerns when I felt the Holy Spirit stop me from speaking. I said hello and walked right past him. *Why did I just do that?*

Every day I hoped Don wouldn't have an issue with my work. It felt like I was walking on eggshells. I would go home exhausted, really hating work for only one reason——Don. One night I had a dream that I was at the station and a terrible hurricane was bearing down. Don and I were the only ones left and as we looked out the window, we knew we could not leave. In my dream, Don said I could stay in his office and we would be safe from the storm. I immediately woke up from this dream and the reality of Don's harshness hit me square in the face.

I went into the office that day and asked Don if I could talk with him. I closed the door and told him about my dream. I said, "Let's say you are going to fire me." Don looked right at me and then looked down at his desk. "Okay," he said slowly.

"I'm asking if you would help me to leave a better person. If you have some suggestions on how I might improve or get better at my work, at least let's work together to assist me as I move on."

Don didn't quite know what to say, but in his most convincing tone he muttered, "You know Laura-Lynn, if you just hang on, this will get better." He told me a story of how he had worked for another show at a different station and hated it, but he kept persevering and it all changed. I tried to feel better after his somewhat odd pep talk. I couldn't put my finger on it, but nothing felt right.

I had some glimmers of light during that time period. For one thing, I received some of the most profound compliments from several sources about my on air work and the level of professionalism to which I had risen. With each compliment that came, I thanked God and wished for things to improve with Don.

On one occasion, I walked by as a director and others were playing back one of my interviews. Suddenly the director noticed I was there and he smiled, stood up and looked right into my eyes and said, "Well done Laura-Lynn!" I said a quiet 'thank you' and walked back to my desk. I had loved the interview too. But even as I celebrated this success, I kept thinking ... *Too bad I won't be here very long.*

I stunned myself with these thoughts. I shook my head as I considered how emotionally difficult working at the studio had become. Even my relationships with the staff had become strained. I felt I was under so much pressure, I asked if I could write my voice-overs at home. Of course, Don said no. It was like sliding downhill with nowhere to place my foot to stop the fall. Once again, I thought about approaching Jack and imploring him to help me. Surely he would hear me and talk to Don. But then I heard this still small voice say, *Don't try to save this.*

What? Why did I hear that? Who was saying this to me: the Holy Spirit or the enemy? *Why can't I stop this? You called me to television and I'm here trying to do Your work, but it looks like I am going to get fired!! Why?*

Things went from bad to worse. Don told me he had gotten another local media talent to do two interviews I was supposed to do. I asked why and he could not give me a reasonable answer. It was so confusing. I the time I would have spent on those interviews to catch up on other work. The skies of my existence just got darker and darker. I now hated going to work. It felt as though the tide had turned against me. I felt rejected and wounded and there was not a thing I seemed to be able to do to change it.

From my vantage point today, I realize I could have let go of the job I was clinging to so tightly. I could have released my grip and trusted God for my future, but I could not comprehend what was happening. I was too fearful to free myself of the agony of that season. I could not see what lay ahead in the future. In truth, had I known I would one day be the host of *The 700 Club Canada*, I would have quit months earlier. God does not reveal the end before the middle. I remained in darkness, simply knowing the tide had shifted.

It was Friday. I always got fired on Fridays. I had just arrived to work when Don asked me to come to Jack's office. I searched my desk, looking at all my things: pictures and memorabilia from interviews I had done, along with all my favorite collectibles from the last five years of my life. This job had helped liberate me from my dark past. *Well, I hope the severance package is good.* I managed a slight smile and then headed down the hallway of doom.

"This is a very black day for the station—a very black day," Jack's face looked drawn and his words hung like daggers in the boardroom. "We are letting you go." My heart raced as I tried to comprehend the fact that what I had feared was coming for months was now an actuality. "You did this, Don!" I blurted out the anger and words I had been holding in for awhile. I pointed at him and told him this was his fault.

I demanded to know why I was being fired. He said the answers would all be in the envelope he handed me. I physically felt a piercing pain in my heart. How could this be happening? Jack looked sick. I felt very angry—angry that I had been hurt, angry that Don had not tried to work with me, angry that he didn't feel I was worth the effort, and angry that I couldn't make sense out of any of this!

I got up, taking my envelope with me. I got my purse from my desk and as is customary, I was escorted out of the building. Don told me in the elevator that he wished the best for me. I could not respond. It was a very devastating moment. My anger was misplaced that day. Little did I realize that God is the One who demotes and promotes. My destiny had never been in Don's hands. He only did what God told him to do. My departure was not his fault. In fact - although it took the better part of two years to understand it—God was preparing me for a promotion.

As I drove away, I took one last glimpse over my shoulder at the building that had once represented a new start, fresh hope, redemption and a God inspired purpose for my life. It drifted out of sight in my rear view mirror as I turned a corner into a monumentally painful, yet profoundly significant time. I felt like Jeremiah in Lamentations 3:1-9 (NKJV):

*I am the man who has seen affliction by the rod of His wrath.*
*He has led me and made me walk*
*In darkness and not in light.*
*Surely He has turned His hand against me*
*Time and time again throughout the day.*
*He has aged my flesh and my skin,*
*And broken my bones.*
*He has besieged me*
*And surrounded me with bitterness and woe.*
*He has set me in dark places*
*Like the dead of long ago.*
*He has hedged me in so that I cannot get out;*
*He has made my chain heavy.*
*Even when I cry and shout,*
*He shuts out my prayer.*
*He has blocked my ways with hewn stone;*
*He has made my paths crooked.*

The first and only thing I knew to do was to get on my knees. I had no tears, which surprised me. I was somewhat numb. By the following morning, I had this knowing in my heart that as difficult as this situation was for me to fathom, it was of God and not of man. As angry as I felt at Don, I truly believed in my heart that he had merely been a pawn in God's plan. I remembered this cherished verse in Habakkuk 3:17-19 (NIV), "Though the fig tree does not bud and there are no grapes on the vines, though the olive crop fails and the fields produce no food, though there are no sheep in the pen and no cattle in the stalls, yet I will rejoice in the LORD, I will be joyful in God my Savior."

I called Jack and asked to meet with him to give him the signed papers accepting the severance package that would get me through the next few months. "Are we still friends, Jack?" I heard him heave a big sigh, "Laura-Lynn, I'm so relieved to hear you say that! I've been sick over this."

When Jack and I met for lunch, the first thing I told him was that this was of God, that it was supposed to happen. I do not know how I knew that, but I knew it was true. All the things I had held in for months came pouring out as Jack listened. It felt better to get it off my chest, even though it didn't change anything. My job there was done.

This was a staggering blow to my life, my pride, and the foundation of my identity. Once again, I was a broken person. *I thought I was past this, God.* My husband, in true form, was strong and unmovable in his belief it would all be okay. His strong arms held me and I was somehow surprised his love didn't seem to waiver one little bit—whether I was a reporter on a cable network or the host on a national TV show.

When you are misunderstood or falsely accused, you are going through one of the key tests you must pass to be ready for substantial use. You must be able to stand in spite of those who would unjustly gossip, misconstrue facts and agendas, misrepresent motives and call into question your integrity. In learning you cannot rely on man's version of reality, God will teach you that He alone is your vindicator. He alone must be your source for truth. This will give you strength beyond measure and prepare you for the road that lies ahead. Remember these words from Galatians 1:10: "Am I now trying to win the approval of human beings, or of God? Or am I trying to please people? If I were still trying to please people, I would not be a servant of Christ"(NIV).

God only tests in this regard, those whom He wants to greatly use, because they will repeatedly be put on the firing line of human judgment and they must be able to stand the heat. Fear of man will make you weak in your call; God will fortify your vessel through the trial of being rejected by others and then having done all, you can stand.

Another strange thing happened that summer. I knew I had been feeling really tired for a long time. It was like a debilitating exhaustion, especially in the final days of working at the station. I had this odd rash under my left eye that I kept putting more and more make-up on to cover. My joints had been inflamed for many years and my hair now began falling out in clumps.

Being so busy, I had simply ignored all of these symptoms and took an aspirin here or there to feel better. But then one day when I woke up, I could not lift the sheet off of me. I went to the doctor and had some tests done. Within a few days, the doctor called me back and asked me to come in right away. I called JT first and he said not to worry, adding "It is never anything!" Of course, he was talking about his own experience in that final comment, as I have often kidded him that he's a hypochondriac and has been tested for everything under the sun, but nothing ever turns up. Symptoms would appear and make him think he had some terrible disease and then when the tests showed that he was perfectly healthy, all the symptoms would disappear.

With his encouragement, I had little fear anything could be seriously wrong. The doctor appeared very calm and professional as she looked me straight in the eyes and said she believed I had lupus, an autoimmune disease. *Wow! That was unexpected. This is tragic news! But wait a minute, what is lupus?*

The doctor assured me that I would be okay, but I would have to be on medication, see a rheumatologist, take more naps, and divide up house chores for the rest of my life. All I heard was that I needed to get more naps and divide up house chores for the rest of my life! How blessed could I be to get a disease that gave me these kinds of perks? I was ecstatic!

She couldn't tell me how I got lupus, but said it could be hereditary. I got on the phone as soon as I left the doctor's office and called JT. I told him that I had a bona-fide disease and needed more rest, less chores and I threw in 'more affection' for good measure. The only thing that JT knew about lupus was that it was the one disease George Costanza, in an episode of *Seinfeld*, had desperately hoped he didn't have.

When I got home, the excitement built in my heart to announce to the family I would need more naps. My kids gathered around and asked what was going on so I told them I had a bona-fide disease and we were going to have to divide up the chores, leaving me with far less to do. I explained I would need a lot more rest.

My youngest son, who was 11 years old at the time, calmly looked at me and said, "Don't think you're getting out of doing dinner tonight." That basically sums up the reaction of my entire family to my bona-fide disease. I don't think I have had any extra naps and about the chores, well, we just all worked to get them done. If I had to do it over again, I would have put a thermometer in my mouth and crawled in from the car. That might have garnered more sympathy. As it is, every time I mention the day I was diagnosed with lupus, the family throws their hands in the air and begins whooping in remembrance!

After the initial treatment to get the lupus under control, my rheumatologist now says I am very blessed because I am doing well and the disease has not affected my internal organs. I've asked if I will stay this well for the rest of my life and the doctor said it is a good possibility. I now realize I have to eat right and get a good amount of rest. I depend on the Holy Spirit every day to remind me to stay on track, which is the very best way to live your life, lupus or no!

# 11

# LONG DESERT NIGHTS

*Burst into songs of joy together, you ruins of Jerusalem, for the Lord has comforted his people, He has redeemed Jerusalem.*

- Isaiah 52:9, NIV

My interviews continued to air for several months. On many nights I had trouble sleeping, so I would wander into the living room with a warm cup of milk and turn on the television. The Biography Channel was re-airing my interviews so I sat there and watched them. My heart ached as I wondered what had gone wrong. I stared at the screen with a critical eye. I watched interview after interview and could not see what would have brought about my dismissal.

Don hired a new host and she was allowed to work from home. She got many courtesies that I was never given. One day, the field producer for the show called me from one of their shoots because the new host wanted to let me know that she was really enjoying (my) job. In all of this, I actually was able to chuckle. There are moments when life gets so bad that you have to wonder if there is something else at work.

I began asking God very intensely why this had happened. *Are You disciplining me?* My mind would go over and over the events leading up to my dismissal. I prayed for clarity, but none came. *God, I'm so sorry. You are obviously angry with me to have let this happen. Please tell me what I have done to displease You so greatly. I will throw myself at Your mercy and beg Your forgiveness, just please let me know what I've done.* God was silent.

Surely this was not the end. How could God have healed my spirit so fully, then called me in 1999 and led me on this miraculous journey through doors that only He could open, just to let the dream die this horrible death in despair and defeat? It didn't make sense. *Where are You, God?* I began making calls to everyone I knew in the media industry. I asked if there were any positions available. I told them I would even make coffee for the hosts if I had to——anything would be fine.

The reality of my plight was sinking in fast. No other miraculous openings appeared. I could not see what God's hand was doing and I certainly could not understand it. *Did You bring me out of Egypt to let me die in this wilderness, Lord?* As I sat again watching the re-runs of my interviews, I cried out to God late one night with my entire being. I could not contain the sorrow any longer.

The rejection was overwhelming. I lay flat on my living room floor with my head buried in the rug. I sobbed over the loss I had experienced. I had hoped that I would be a new creation; a new person with a new name and a new destiny. Who was I now without all the lights, camera, and action? I realized my position had come to mean a tremendous amount to me. In my mind, it symbolized my value and worth. I was a somebody because of what I did. I was a performer and if I performed well, then I was loved. If I failed at my performance, I feared that I would no longer be loved. The magnitude of this under-standing swept over me as the tears flowed. *Who am I now, God?*

I'm not sure why God has continually used Disney movies to teach me lessons during different times of my life. Because deep inside I still felt like a little girl looking for her worth, I guess sometimes a cartoon says it all. As I lay there, a picture of Pride Rock from the movie *The Lion King* appeared before my eyes.

Pride Rock was a large and beautiful rock ledge that protruded from the mountainside in a majestic outcropping on a Kenyan land-scape. I saw myself hanging over the edge, only being held by a fraying rope around my waist. The following gentle whisper of conversation was the only thing I heard from God in this desert experience. As my tears made a puddle on my carpet, I heard my Friend, who is closer than a brother, speak to my heart, *Do you trust Me in this dark place, where the only One who can catch you is Me? Will you trust Me in the darkness? For if you will not trust Me in the barren places, I will not be able to trust you in the spacious places.*

I felt the gentle breeze of Jesus flow over my soul and I perceived that His question demanded an answer. Kneeling prostrate to the ground, with the intensity of a wounded warrior, I raised my fist in the air and pounded on my living room floor for all I was worth, "I trust You. I trust You. I trust You!" I got louder with each hit and finally declared, "Though You slay me, yet will I trust You!!"

I breathed deeply as the pressure of all the rejection, failure, worry and pain I had experienced left my being. Once again, surrender was the only thing God asked of me. There was nothing else for me to do but relinquish my hopes, dreams, insecurities and defeat to Him. During this act of contrition, I found the peace I had been searching for. *I was free!*

I discovered that when something ends in your life, it is so God can make room for a new thing. As I look back, I see that I had to let go of dreams I valued in order for an even better plan to be launched. We cannot hold onto what we think is best. We must trust the Creator because His idea is way better than ours.

I also found one other beautiful thing. The desert has flowers so stunning, you may one day look back and miss what that dry, parched journey brought you. For me, the flowers were the beauty of God's breast to rest upon when there was no consolation on earth to alleviate the pain; the small comforts of my child's smile when the larger comforts like a paycheck had vanished; the realization of truth and the letting go of a counterfeit; the tiny glimpses of glory that hinted at hope coming; the passing of tests that would form a foundation to hold the unquenchable power of God.

God could not tell me the future and relieve the intensity of the firing kiln. The refining of the gold that lies within us only comes through the pain of adversity. The impurities need to be heated out of the crevices where they hide. They can then rise to the surface and be removed. Our character will become hardened, like a core metal, which will not bend or break under the weight of all God's destiny will need us to bear.

God uses closed doors to launch us into our next promotion. At first glance, a closed door is disappointing, especially if it seemed that specific door was surely the one to usher in our purpose. As I look back and consider the key moments that led to my greatest successes, they were all predicated by shut doors, locked doors, barred and slammed-in-my-face doors.

Yet, without those closed doors, I would never be where I am today - and I love today! If you are at an impasse, standing in front of a door that will not open no matter how hard you bang on it, get down on your knees and give thanks! You are one door closer to the greatest moment of your life, when the entryway you have been longing for will swing open with such intensity and power that no man will be able to close it!

I was once again facing my inadequate understanding of who I was. Yes, I knew I was forgiven at the cross and I now had no shame. Yes, I knew I was of royal heritage adopted by God into His family. Nothing could change that! I could now claim key verses that gave my soul strength.

I knew, according to John 15:16, that I was chosen by God, "You didn't choose me. I chose you. I appointed you to go and produce lasting fruit, so that the Father will give you whatever you ask for, using my name" (NLT). I really wanted to produce lasting fruit. I wanted to perform well, finish the race set before me, press towards the mark of the high calling of God and see the promise of 2 Corinthians 9:8, "And God is able to bless you abundantly, so that in all things at all times, having all that you need, you will abound in every good work" (NIV).

But I had no work. What if the lasting fruit was *surrender*? I was left to sit on my living room floor, being torched by the kiln. I didn't like it! The issue God needed to deal with in my life was my lifelong need to please others and to perform so I would be loved, admired and cherished. God had now stripped me of the small trophies I had earned. Who was I then? I honestly did not know. The only thing I knew was that I had to trust God and God alone. I had no accomplishments to hang my hat on, not any more; they had all developed wings and flown away.

Life will inevitably present us with the opportunity to be angry, not just with people, but even God himself. We can be angry about our circumstances, losses and troubles. Some have uttered their blame towards God for the calamities that befall the planet. Some who get angry at Him, barely believe in Him. There are two ways to deal with the inevitable pain and failure: trust God or blame God. The outcomes are different. One will lead to healing and wholeness, the other to bitterness, further agony and resentment.

It must be noted that some people cause their own chaos and are completely blind to their culpability. They do not walk in wisdom, obedience, righteousness or holiness and then when it all caves in, they blame God. Proverbs 19:3 speaks of this, "A man's own folly ruins his life, yet his heart rages against the LORD" (NIV84). It is difficult to rage at God and also receive His peace, His power and His goodness.

Anger at God is always misplaced and will only lead to further resentment and quite literally, an unstable mindset. The enemy of your soul knows very well that if you resent your God, you do not trust

Him. You are practicing atheism when you cannot trust the hand of your Father in heaven. Faith will change everything; it is an act of your will. We have an example to follow in the life of Job. After all the disasters happened to him, we see in Job 1:22, "In all this Job sinned not nor charged God foolishly" (KJV).

When God asked me to trust Him that night on the carpet, I had to choose to do it. I could have continued to mourn the loss of my dreams and hopes or I could put my faith in the Creator of the universe. When God puts a dream in your heart, He begins the process of getting you ready for that destiny. This involves crushing your ego, pruning your attitudes, shaping your feisty spirit, breaking your willful soul, and molding your character into the beautiful vessel that you were created to be.

Ironically, it is a powerful sign of your impending promotion and the supernatural release of your destiny, when you realize you are not talented or smart enough to make it happen. It is in the recognition of your limitations that you will be liberated to rely on a power greater than yourself. What God has designed for your future will take far more than He naturally equipped your body, soul and spirit with. It will take complete surrender to the power of the Holy Spirit.

When you finally resign yourself to the futility of relying on your own strength and in your weakness you cry out for Heaven's assistance, in that very moment, God is able to launch you into a greater call than you ever dreamed possible. Though it may feel as if it is admitting failure, surrender is actually the most formidable weapon you can add to your arsenal for the journey.

SOLID ROCK
CHRISTIAN FELLOWSHIP

Prior to this epiphany, you may have done it all in your own strength, thereby severely reducing your capabilities. The larger territory that awaits you cannot be conquered by human skill, perfection, performance or presentation. It takes the hand of God Almighty to make it happen. Realizing you need Him to bring about your extraordinary purpose is the most profound lesson you may ever learn. *You, plus God, equals amazing!*

In spite of all that had happened, a newfound peace and joy entered my spirit. I was at complete rest with it all. I started applying for jobs everywhere - administrative work, charities, churches, warehouses, anywhere I thought I would be a good fit. I kept thinking that surely someone would hire me. I'm a good worker. I'm loyal, honest and highly motivated. But no one called me back.

Time was getting short and our money was going to run out in two weeks. I placed my head down on the newspaper ad section and prayed. There was one tiny, inconspicuous ad asking for homes for high-risk youth. I had grown up with my parents taking in anyone who needed help, from oversees students to families in some kind of transition. We always had an open door policy for those in need. I called the number and left a message saying that we would be happy to do this.

The next morning, a representative from the organization called and explained the program to me. I invited her to come over and see our home to assess whether we would be a good fit. She explained that the kids we would be getting were straight from the youth jail and they would spend the final four months of their sentence with us. For some reason, I was thrilled! As it stood, no one seemed interested in hiring me for anything. The paycheck we received from caring for these kids was exactly the right amount we needed to make ends meet. Without missing one payday, we transitioned into caring for young people who had seen desperate times. God again proved that His timing was impeccable and His faithfulness a surety for life.

The first kid who came to our home was Will. He spent four months with us and we embraced his beautiful spirit. He loved our home and told his friends he lived in a mansion and ate like a king. He was from First Nations and had lost communication with both his parents. When we first took Will to church, he told us he had been there before. Since Will was from Lillooet, a small town in the interior of British Columbia some four hours away, I asked if he was sure he had been to this particular church. He said a friend of his dad's used to bring them. He glanced up at me and said, "Maybe my dad is here?"

During the following weeks, we kept a look out for Will's dad. As we entered church one Sunday night, I said, "Will, we are going to need a miracle. We will have to pray that we find your dad or someone who knows him." During the service that night, Will tapped me on the shoulder and pointed to a man a few rows over, "He's the man who used to bring us to church here." After the service, I practically hopped over pews to get to the fellow, and indeed Will was right. This man had brought them to church a couple years back when Will had spent a little time with his dad, William Sr.

"Do you know where William is by any remote chance?" I asked, not thinking the man would possibly have that information.

"Yes, I know exactly where he works and where he lives." *That is crazy,* I thought! I gave the man my cell number and asked if he would pass it on to William Sr.

I was sweeping my kitchen floor when William called the next day! He had a great voice and infectious personality. I was surprised and so happy that Will could reunite with his dad. What a miracle!

Will and I met William at an Alcoholics Anonymous meeting that week. He was so happy to see Will. He had a wonderful smile and tattoos of a spider that crawled up his neck and down his arms. We talked after the meeting and William told us how he wanted to be an actor or direct a movie.

William was staying on track with AA and was a great example for his son. One day I asked William if he had a personal relationship with Jesus. I was surprised by his response because I knew he had taken Will to the church we now attended. William informed me that he thought all 'gods' were fine and he wasn't narrowing it down to Jesus. When I told him that there was no other name under heaven by which man can be saved, he became annoyed.

Time went on and I loved seeing father and son together. The beauty of this reunion was even more powerful when William invited Will to come and live with him, instead of returning to his small town. It was a perfect story until about three weeks before Will's graduation from the program. William relapsed and went back to Main and Hastings——Canada's worst street for addicts.

When I heard this news from one of William's friends, I sobbed in my living room. My heart could not bear the pain. Will was looking forward to living with his dad. Later that same day, some horrible news came that a young man who had recently graduated from this program had overdosed on heroine. Within days, we all attended his funeral and I could see the look of fear and pain in Will's eyes.

There were many reports in the news that a bad strain of heroin was in the city—many were overdosing and dying. William was a heroin addict. We didn't know it yet, but even as we heard the news reports, William was in the hospital being brought back to life from an overdose. In addition to this new heroine addiction, William was an alcoholic and had previously been introduced to cocaine. He said the only thing that cocaine makes you want is more cocaine.

William wanted to make lots of money fast, so in his younger days he started doing armed robberies. One time, he took the ten-year-old daughter of the owner of a convenience store hostage and ordered the owner to open up the safe, stating no one would get hurt if he cooperated. His co-conspirator was in the getaway car waiting for him. Once the owner emptied the safe, William dragged the young girl to the door and let her go as he raced to the car. Unfortunately, his accomplice had gotten out to relieve himself behind the building and another thief stole their car. William and his accomplice ran for what seemed miles until K9 dogs picked up their scent and they were arrested and taken to jail.

Nothing could deter William from his life of rebellion, lawlessness and crime. He committed fraud, dealt drugs, pimped and committed many robberies. He eventually spent a total of eight years in jail and finally came to the end of himself through the humiliation of being treated like an animal. At that point, he desperately cried out for something more.

His father had been a devout Christian after his own struggles with alcohol. He lined the walls of their home with pictures of Jesus and told William that Jesus was the way, the truth and the life, and that he needed to turn his life over to Christ. William only scoffed at his father and grew to hate himself and his life. He questioned how God could let such terrible things happen to him. He became abusive to those in his life and was swallowed up with misery, depression and anxiety. Even the birth of his two sons, Will and Ryan, did not bring his rage to an end. He defiantly continued his destructive ways—cussing out anyone who would ever cross him.

Those years brought William some terrible street beatings and nine overdoses; he was stabbed and left to die a hopeless drug addict. By sheer will and determination, he made his way to an AA meeting and found sobriety. He pulled himself from decay for a season. That's when I met him—when he was two years clean. But now William had suffered a relapse.

Amazingly to me, William came back from his relapse and said he had made a big mistake and he was sorry. He assured me that it wouldn't happen again. I was very naïve about addiction, so I was over-joyed at his assurances. I was sure this had just been a big mistake and William had come to his senses for good now.

We secured a job for Will upon graduation as a dishwasher for a well-known restaurant. All the pieces of his life were falling perfectly into place. The night before Will's graduation, I was unable to reach William. He didn't answer his phone. I kept thinking that he was probably just busy doing something, but I never heard from him.

The next day, Will had a small pocketknife in his jacket. He pulled it out to show another kid in the program and one of the workers saw it. Will was not allowed to have weapons and so he lost his right to have a graduation celebration. The center called me before the graduation to let me know about the situation. I tried to call William to inform him of what happened. I called and called, but there was no answer. I finally contacted a woman he had been seeing. She bluntly, with a resigned tone said, "He's gone out again, Laura-Lynn. He's using drugs. I know the signs; I can't reach him either."

I headed for the center where Will was being released. Upon arriving, I looked into the sad eyes of this young man who had now been segregated to the boardroom downstairs. He was told that his dad was not coming to his graduation. There was such despondency in his demeanor; it broke my heart. I spoke with my voice cracking, "Will, I'm so sorry. This is not the end. You will survive this. You must decide to do the right things in life, even if others fail you. You need to choose today to keep going on the right track—no matter what. You have a destiny, Will! Don't let anyone take it from you." He could only nod. I fought back the tears and said goodbye.

William contacted me later that day to apologize. He was sorry for not having been there for Will. I could hear the pain in his voice, but it was too late. I felt so angry inside and told him about having to look in Will's eyes and see the anguish—— anguish that was there because he knew his dad was not coming. There was desperation in William's voice, but now that Will was gone, I never wanted to speak to William again. I refused all of his calls and attempts to contact me. I was done with him—but God wasn't!

One year later, a wonderful thing happened. Ryan, Will's little brother, was now coming through the program and ironically, he was headed to our house. Quite a series of miraculous events had to line-up in order for him to be placed with us. In my heart, I felt this was no random happening. Ryan was meant to be at our home. What a sense of humor this kid had! He also loved chicken, just like his older brother. Since cooking was not my specialty, it was really cool that both of these guys liked the one thing I cooked the most—rice and chicken!

During the four months that Ryan stayed with us, beautiful things happened. Will moved back to our area on his own and we were able to see him at recovery meetings. The first time we went up to meet with him, I realized I had given Will the wrong address at which to meet us. After searching for him on foot, Ryan and I got back into the van and set out to find him. I had no idea where to begin looking, so Ryan, knowing my faith, told me to pray. I prayed out loud several times, "God, You know where Will is. Please let us find him."

I drove almost in a trance, turning down streets in an indiscriminate way. We hadn't driven more than five minutes when Ryan suddenly yelled, "There he is!" The boys greeted each other excitedly as they each commented on how messed up my directions were and how very strange it was that they had found each other in this big city. Ryan said, "We prayed man!" I loved these kids and it brought tears to my eyes to see them so happy and safe.

We met as often as we could and took Will food when he didn't have any in his cupboards. We also found out that their dad was once again doing well—clean and sober. We met up with him at the Narcotics Anonymous meeting and I put aside my grudge and embraced him as their father. There was something striking about William's spirit. He had married a lovely Christian woman and was baptized in church. It was a beautiful thing to watch these wonderful boys reunited with their dad on good terms. Young Will had walked down to the front of a church on two different occasions and given his life to God.

Needless to say, the demon of addiction was still licking at William's back and he relapsed again. He spent 13 days straight, sitting in the heart of Vancouver's worst area. He saw a man murdered with whom he had done crack cocaine. Then another man died right in front of him. The stench of death and addiction on the streets began to overwhelm him. He heard the sounds of people screaming at each other with foul language and hatred in their hearts.

He saw mice running around eating rotten food. The smell of alcohol made him sick. He was homeless. His marriage was over and all was lost. He had always been a dreamer and had hoped to make something of his life, but the methods and lifestyle he chose left him broken, empty and alone.

William continued to use crack cocaine, heroine and anything else he could get his hands on, but this time nothing stopped the ache in his heart. The drugs were not able to relieve the emotional pain from the loss of his relationships and emptiness of his life. We can run from God, but William's life has shown me, we can't hide. God loved this man since his conception and had crafted his destiny.

Finally, something inside of William broke. He knew he would be the next to die where he was, in the notorious Pigeon Park, if he did not find a way to change. As his life began to ebb away, with hope seeping from every pore, two men from Teen Challenge walked up to him and noticed that he didn't look good. They asked if he needed help and took him to a shelter. William could hear the men of Teen Challenge asking for him to be put at the front of the line for help because his situation looked grave.

William never knew their names, but they rescued his soul that day. Perhaps only in heaven will the identities of these two men be revealed—these good Samaritans reaching out to a poor, desperate addict, in whose life they cared to intervene. Since that day, William's life was forever changed and he has never gone back. In a moment of absolute desperation, William cried out to the God who had walked with him down every backstreet alley and rescued him from every overdose. The Friend who had whispered his name and called him from shame, was there to receive this son who had walked so far away.

This time, William's voice called out to Jesus. He remembered what I said, just like his dad had told him, *Jesus is the way, the truth and the life.* William needed that life. In a frantic place, along a path that had almost been lost, he found the one true hope that would rescue his soul for the final time from disaster and addiction. From that point on, he would never be the same. The next time I saw William, he had a glow about him that has not left to this day!

William, with his wonderful laugh and extraordinary spirit, is one of the most inspiring people I have ever known. The work that Jesus did in taking a lost soul from the most deplorable places, like Main and Hastings in Vancouver, and elevating him to a stable and profound place of influence in our community, has been one of the most incredible things I have ever personally witnessed in my life.

I helped William find a basement suite for him and Ryan to live in when he graduated from the program. We drove around one evening for about five hours, going from place to place. When people saw that William had many tattoos, they were not too eager to rent to him. Finally, we went to the last basement suite on our list and I looked in the landlord's eyes and said, "I guarantee these will be great tenants, please give this a shot." I gave him my personal phone number and sent a quick prayer upwards. The landlords, two brothers, seemed apprehensive—looking down a lot and glancing at each other with questions in their eyes. They finally said, "Okay, we'll do it." *It was a miracle!*

William and Ryan soon moved in and Will came to live with them as well. I looked forward to my daily calls from William to talk about this amazing turn of events. He called with parenting questions and talked about how his life had been radically changed by his faith in Jesus Christ. He marveled at how things fell into place as he prayed about everything. William never hung up without thanking me and conveying how their family's lives had changed forever because of our meeting. I always laughed at his kind words. William called me "Lyn-skers" and I called him "Willis." Our friendship has been one of my most treasured relationships to this day.

Several times Will and Ryan gave up drinking completely, but would find the addiction too much of a temptation and fall back into it. At Christmastime 2008, I was so excited to get them some gifts. I received a call on my cell phone from Ryan and Will thanking me for the gifts. I didn't know that was the last time I would ever speak to Will.

# 12
# PEACE LIKE A RIVER

*Into Your hands I commit my spirit; You have redeemed me, O*
*Lord, the God of truth and faithfulness.*

- Psalm 31:5

I love the song, "It Is Well with My Soul." Consider these words
from the first verse of that song.

*When peace like a river attendeth my way,*
*When sorrows like sea billows roll;*
*Whatever my lot, Thou hast taught me to say,*
*It is well, it is well, with my soul.*

I love the story behind how this beautiful hymn was penned. The
author, Horatio Spafford, had it all in the 1800s. He was a wealthy
Chicago lawyer with a beautiful wife, a four-year-old son, four wonderful daughters and a lovely home. He was a strong man of faith
who hung out with the likes of D.L. Moody and he loved to study the
scriptures.

Within a short span of time, his young son died suddenly and
the Chicago Fires completely decimated his financial portfolio. As if
matters couldn't get any worse, he sent his wife and daughters off on
a ship travelling to Europe in order for them to grieve their loss and

find some rest. Their vessel was hit by another ship and it sank quickly, killing all four of his daughters. His wife later sent him a now well-known telegram, which only said, "Saved alone".

Several days later, Spafford, in the most incredible storm of his personal life, wrote the time-treasured words of this hymn. "Though Satan should buffet, though trials should come, let this blest assurance control, that Christ has regarded my helpless estate and hath shed his own blood for my soul. It is well with my soul." Spafford was a man truly at peace, trusting Jesus with his helpless, powerless position. Later his wife and he had three more children—two girls and a boy - but their son died in infancy.

It had been a really tough year for some friends of mine. One woman lost her husband very quickly to cancer within eight days of hearing the diagnosis. Another couple lost their beautiful 15-year-old son overnight to meningitis. The same day of this loss, Cam and Janine held their hands to heaven and declared their trust in God. Their faith inspired my soul. As we gathered at their home over the next several days, I had never witnessed such grief and at the same time, such over-whelming peace from the Father.

Thinking about such unimaginable pain, I only pray that God would find me on my knees in surrender to His will. *Father, may our lives exude such trust, such dependence on You, that whatever our lot, we will live and breathe in the knowledge that You are faithful and we can trust You. It is well with my soul.*

I had scheduled lunch with a girlfriend about 30 minutes from my place. On the way to lunch, I complained to myself for arranging to drive this distance when I needed to write and study for a speaking engagement that night at a youth event. It was good to see Nancy and we talked about some big changes she was feeling she needed to make. I looked down at my cell phone and realized I had missed a call from William. He had left an unsettling message that the police were looking for him and needed to speak to him personally. He said he was worried the boys had done something bad and were possibly in trouble.

During lunch, I had not read the news feed on my Blackberry. The feed reported the murder of a 19-year-old youth in Vancouver. When William called again towards the end of our lunch, I told Nancy this was his second call and I needed a moment to take it. William's voice was broken, "Laura-Lynn, Will is dead; he's been murdered!" I stared at my plate and covered my other ear in an attempt to hear over the noise of the restaurant. I thought I'd heard William say that Will was dead... "What William?"

"Will is dead. The police just told me he was murdered last night!" he said again.

I couldn't believe what I was hearing, "Are you sure William? Will is dead?" William would sometimes play jokes on me and I almost hoped, as awful as this was, that somehow he was just kidding me right now. There seemed no way to comprehend what he was saying. "Oh my God, oh my God, are you sure William? I'm so sorry, this can't be true." I started to cry and asked where he was. Thankfully he was just two blocks from where I was having lunch.

Nancy prayed with me and asked God to bring His peace to this situation. I left in shock and disbelief that life could deal such a tragic blow. I pulled to the curb to pick up William as he was clinging to his computer. He had been on his way to a downtown computer store to have it serviced when the police met with him to give him this life altering news. His face was etched with grief and he stood motionless at the curb.

I looked quickly at the many people bustling by and thought how very strange it was that this father stood there with the worst possible news about the death of his son and yet just a few feet from him, folks went on about their business with no knowledge of his pain. As he got into the vehicle, I realized I had no idea what to say to a father who was suffering such loss. My stomach ached and my heart hurt. *What must William be feeling, knowing he would never embrace his son again?* We drove away in silence for a moment and then in broken patterns of speech we tried to go over what the police had said.

Will was murdered in east Vancouver, at a party gone wrong. He was actually defending Ryan's girlfriend from an older member of the gang they ran with. Always chivalrous, Will stood up to stop an inappropriate move by this guy and was knifed five times. As Will lay there dying, the perpetrator took the girl out and raped her. Nothing made sense. Tears ran down our faces. I didn't know where I was driving. *Where would we go?*

I thought about my Pastor, Mike Poulin. He would know what to do. He had just performed the funeral for another family in our church whose son was gunned down in his driveway in a gang related shooting earlier that week.

Pastor Mike dropped everything and told us to go to a nearby restaurant where we spent a couple of hours trying to comfort a grieving dad. William had so many questions. Where was Will? He hadn't been in the right place. He hadn't been doing the right things. He certainly hadn't been hanging with the right people. Where was he? Was he with Jesus even though he had been in the wrong place at the wrong time?

We talked with Pastor Mike about Will's conversion, twice having given his life to Jesus during his stay at my home. Will had even attended church by himself about two months before. A tremendous comfort began to settle over us as we talked. I had this sense that God had Will. He was marked and set apart, even though he wasn't perfect. A calm knowing overtook my spirit. Adoption into Christ's family was sealed by a blood relationship with Him that surpassed mere mortal actions in a moment of time.

William had no immediate family to go to. I was the closest thing to family he would have that day, so he came with me to my speaking engagement that night. There was no hiding the tragedy. I told the audience of youth who gathered about the devastating events that had occurred over the past 24 hours. William allowed me to share a piece of the story, even as he sat in the pew. There was a silent hush over the auditorium as we all experienced a moment of clarity on the brevity of life and the need for sobriety in body and soul. What a mere whisper this earthly existence is. Can we possibly understand how delicate, how easily extinguished this flame could be, with only a heartbeat between time and eternity?

Will's funeral was somber and it was noted several times by different speakers that Will had sacrificed himself in defense of another. Seeing Ryan under these circumstances was strangely comforting because at least he was alive so there was hope for him. He hugged me and wouldn't let go for a long time. He told his dad that he would change. Some of Will and Ryan's friends had gone to a Bible study the night before and were hungry for answers about life. They had an open casket and as I stood staring at the beautiful face of Will, my heart ached.

Today, William has forgiven his son's murderer and says that even if this man were to end up right in his path, he would lead him to know Jesus. He never relapsed through this most difficult loss. His testimony is astounding and his life is a beacon of hope to every crumbling and desperate soul who no longer believes they have worth.

William is employed full-time as the program coordinator of a recovery home and is able to share his incredible story of redemption and forgiveness every day. William and I have remained true friends, speaking every week. He is in love with a beautiful Christian woman and they are getting married next year.

Relentless redemption pursued an addict others gave up on a long, long time ago. It dared to travel down evil-laden alleys, hover in dark doorways where needles were cradled like gold, and it oversaw the work of an emergency doctor's hands when a life hung in the balance after an overdose.

Shining through the blackest of depravity, redemption is the light that calls to a derelict sinner to come home to a merciful God who never stops believing we were created for a stunning purpose. William stands as the truest example I have known of a life redeemed, freed and liberated from what should have been his destruction.

When you are facing a significant challenge or trial in your life, you can be sure that God knows exactly what you are going through. He is fully aware of your situation even if you do not feel His presence and cannot hear His voice. God will work this situation for good in your life. It may look like a disaster today, but God takes everything the devil means for evil and turns it into good. It may take a while, but you will live to see the day when you thank God for the lessons learned in this desert season. God will never leave you or forsake you. He is closer than the air you breathe and He loves you more than you will ever comprehend. You can trust Him!

During a fiery trial, stay on your knees, giving it to God and surrendering yourself to the process that God has for you. Surrendering is relinquishing your expectations, desires and dreams to His will and becoming content in whatever state you find yourself. Walk in complete obedience to even the smallest thing He asks of you. If God asks you to let go of something you're desperately holding onto, maybe a dream or an unfilled hope in your heart, just let it go. God will sort it out for your good. If the Word says you need to forgive the one who has offended you, then forgive.

When you face a challenge that has brought you to the end of yourself, be silent before God. When Jesus faced the most horrendous experience of His earthly life, right before He went to the cross, He said in John 14:30 (NKJV), "I will no longer talk much with you, for the ruler of this world is coming, and he has nothing in Me." The trial Jesus was facing would ultimately bring salvation and freedom to mankind for all of eternity. He knew He had to bear down and draw strength from the Father alone. The Word says in Lamentations 3:26 and 28, "It is good that one should hope and wait quietly for the salvation of the Lord. Let him sit alone and keep silent." The Message version phrases verse 28 this way, "When life is heavy and hard to take, go off by yourself. Enter the silence. Bow in prayer. Don't ask questions: Wait for hope to appear."

One of the single most beneficial disciplines of our lives is to learn to be silent and wait for God to speak. If we can master this, we will experience less anxiety and fear and have more focus and clarity on issues that pervade us. We will develop a closer relationship with Him. God speaks to us, but with all the noise of our busy schedules - our iPods, iPhones, iPads and TV shows - how on earth can we hear Him? Jesus told His disciples in Matthew 6:6 (MSG), "Find a quiet, secluded place so you won't be tempted to role-play before God. Just be there as simply and honestly as you can manage. The focus will shift from you to God, and you will begin to sense his grace."

We have a promise that whatever we face, God knows exactly who we are and what we are going through. He is very capable and invested in seeing us come through the circumstance, trial or battle in victory. We are not alone; we are not forgotten. Even though the silence may seem deafening and dark clouds may loom, the Word declares that He will never leave us, never forsake us. Deuteronomy 1:31 says, "In the wilderness… you saw how the LORD your God carried you, as a man carries his son, in all the way that you went until you came to this place" (NKJV) My Heavenly Father carried me, though I could not see Him with my earthly eyes. He sustained me through the desert.

He hems us in before and behind. Have no doubt that He is working behind the scenes, orchestrating your deliverance, designing your vindication, carrying the weight of the burden until it is released and the battle is over. Stand fast on His promise, not on your feelings or fear. When you do this, you will release His power. According to your faith, be it unto you. He is a God of power, tremendous might, inexplicable strength and unending compassion. He is on your side. Isaiah 45:2-3 states, "I will go before you and will level the mountains; I will break down gates of bronze and cut through bars of iron. I will give you hidden treasures, riches stored in secret places, so that you may know that I am the LORD, the God of Israel, who summons you by name" (NIV).

The biggest mistake you can make when you feel God has gone silent is to think He is not strategically and intentionally engaged in crafting your next assignment. When God sees you remaining faithful, sound, committed, and undeterred in your devotion to Him, He knows you are trustworthy and ready for the promotion He has miraculously designed for you.

The Master Architect knows you must be strong enough to handle what is coming your way. He will break off your pride, self-will and false identity. When He sees you bow in submission, not in anger, to whatever His will is, He will release the locks on the doors that have been shut. Then the silence ends and His magnificent plan is unveiled. You will see more than you imagined could transpire. Silence sometimes means that God is preparing a surprise for you. Be patient and trust Him.

You cannot earn God's love; You already have it. You cannot make yourself righteous. He is your righteousness. You do not need to promote yourself. He will lead you to better places than you could have dreamed. He is your all in all. He is everything you will ever need—the sum total of all achievement. There is a rest that can be entered, even though you can't understand what God is doing.

Life was moving along at a normal, steady pace. We had many more youth in our home and it was an amazing joy for us to invest in their lives. I loved it and still do! In fact it was so fulfilling that I found that I could see myself doing this without hosting on television again. The sense of purpose I felt in giving kids a safe home had been an unforeseen blessing to my soul.

It was during this time that the lovely Lorna Dueck came to our area and held an evening of fund raising for her television show *Context*. This show took the news events of the day and revealed the incredible way God had woven His hand into and through the stories. She once visited Channel 10 while I was working there and it had been such a privilege for me to drive this amazing woman to her hotel one evening. I shared my heart with her on that trip; it was a conversation I had never forgotten. I revered her as a mentor and woman who had paved the way for Christian television.

I decided to attend her event at the request of another good friend, Maralee Dawn, who would prove to play a significant role in my life in the days to come. Lorna shared her heart and vision to capture the real stories behind some of the nightly news clips. I felt a sting of jealousy in my heart as I realized she was taking God's work to the nation through the venue of television. I thought I had that call, but now here I was, fired and sitting on the shelf.

I quietly repented for having this kind of emotion rise up within my heart. I had declared I would trust God, and if I did, then there was no room for the envy of others. I loved Lorna's heart. She was a tenacious woman who raised her own support for the program God had placed in her heart. I felt a rush of God's power go through me as I gave into her work. The negative emotions were broken.

I knew God had tested my heart. He had put a person before my eyes who was doing the very thing I could only dream of doing. God wanted to know if I would love and not hate, bless and not curse, act rightly or allow a jealous spirit to steal my peace on a day when I could not see God ever opening another door.

That evening Lorna spoke with me and said she believed I was in a season of maturing and preparation to be used again. Those were beautiful words and I received them into my spirit, albeit I could not see any possibility or movement on God's part. In my attempts to find the will of God, it seemed another opportunity was presenting itself through a friend.

Lorna had enlisted the help of an acting agent and suggested I give that a try. Maybe God would open a completely new door for me to be an actor. I arrived early to meet the woman who owned the talent agency. I had a few minutes before our meeting and so I sat there in my car praying for God's favor and grace over my life. I asked Him to open doors that no man could shut and to move on my behalf in power. I certainly hadn't been able to do anything without Him.

I felt prompted to write a prayer or a vision down in my agenda book. Habakkuk 2:2 instructs us to make the vision plain, so that everyone who reads it may run with it, or help you accomplish it. I wrote, *My Father, help my heart to be steadfast towards You…I ask You, Father, for national and international influence…that I might make a difference to the hurting, the broken and the wounded.* I felt faith rise up inside me while writing this declaration of confidence in God. It was as if I could feel the presence of the Lord inspiring me to write a larger vision than my heart thought possible. I could feel His anointing so strongly!

Not one good thing came from the meeting with that talent agency—except that prayer! I managed to get myself stuck in a series of embarrassing auditions, which yielded nothing but the surety that I was not destined to be an actor. Remember, I couldn't even memorize lines. This was definitely not a good fit for me! I would walk in front of the producers who were looking for that 'right' person and I would bumble and jumble off something that wasn't even in the script and then look down and leave quickly.

I remember many times walking back to my vehicle thinking *What on earth am I doing?* I took the prayer I wrote that day and I read it repeatedly; I quoted it and prayed it again and again. *God use my life; take me to places I could not dream possible.* I sometimes wondered what incredible vision I was hoping would come to pass. Yet, I had known the hand of God to move powerfully over my life and lift me out of a dungeon and set me in a spacious place, so there was this knowing in my "knower" that God could indeed do anything He wanted to.

I got in contact with Margaret Gibb and Marilyn Bussey who both worked for a national women's organization. I sent them an email expressing my longing to serve women in some capacity. I received a quick response and they let me know that they would be in Kelowna visiting some family members. I called my mom and dad to see if they wanted to make the trip with me, and of course, my wonderful parents drove me to meet with the ladies for lunch.

These great women helped me organize a women's team in our area. It was so fulfilling to serve in this capacity. Our Vancouver team brought in the delightful Carol Kent as a speaker for our women's event and it was amazing to watch this woman of God breathe life and hope into the audience. She was such an inspiration to me. It was a privilege to emcee at the event.

Later, I travelled to Edmonton to emcee a Women Alive event with incredible speaker and author Pam Farrel. She is one of the funniest ladies I have ever seen on stage. Pam and I flew back to Vancouver together. After I realized she was going to Vancouver, I paid the penalty to switch flights so I could fly with her. It was the best $50 I have ever spent, to be that close to a woman who has authored over 25 books. I asked questions non-stop for two hours and she poured out a wealth of knowledge and insight on publishing and writing.

We also brought in the irresistible Thelma Wells, formerly of Women of Faith. Emceeing for her was like being with a legend. She has authored six books and has mentored women all over the world, speaking to crowds of thousands. I was floored to be in the company of these outstanding women time and again. I couldn't believe God's blessing. Even though I felt insignificant, He kept putting me on stage with the most prolific and powerful women of our generation.

I kept praying and asking for God to use me and enlarge my territory, even in this broken season. I asked Him to rescue me according to Psalm 18:19, "He brought me out into a spacious place; he rescued me because he delighted in me" (NIV). I wanted God to delight in me. I pressed in like never before to have an intimate and powerful relationship with Him. I knew that nothing else mattered. I realized that losing my job at the station had forced me to pursue God more relentlessly, which led me to find ways to serve Him that I never would have found if I had my cushy job at the station.

One day I began thinking about the private producer funds available for programming through the station where I had previously worked. You could not be an employee and access them but if you were not employed, then perhaps they might be available. I thought long and hard about who was the most interesting and energizing person I had worked with at the station. There was no doubt in my mind—it was Mark Washington.

At that time Mark was the First Safety for the British Columbia Lions Canadian Football League football team. He came into the station to shoot some fun segments that followed a comedy about a professional basketball player. We had to banter back and forth for about two to three minutes after each show. He had such a charismatic, easy-going, quick wit. He was also brilliant on camera. There was just something about his love for God and commitment to all that was good. It was inspiring.

I remember feeling strongly that if I could ever pick a co-host for a show, Mark would be the guy! When I approached him with the idea, he told me to put it together. I felt compelled to write out a treatment to present to the station to see if they would consider it. I spent a few hours coming up with a morning show type concept in which Mark and I could chat back and forth while interviewing guests.

I added pictures of us that had already been taken from the segments we had done together in the past. I also included our bios, which for Mark had a magnificent Grey Cup win attached. I then sent this information off to Jack to see if he was interested. One day, I got a call from him and he seemed pretty positive about my idea.

I didn't hear back from Jack again so I finally called him. He told me that the idea wasn't going to fly. He didn't think the duo would work with a Canadian audience and there was no interest from the station. As I said good-bye and hung up the phone, I thought, *I must have no spiritual discernment, because I could have sworn the Holy Spirit gave me that idea.* It was exhausting to have hopes and to keep trying with no results.

The worst part was I felt this hunger inside to do television again, but it seemed that God was clearly showing me He was done with me in that venue. Have you ever felt in your heart that God had given you the go ahead to pursue an opportunity, walk into a promotion or take a territory of destiny in your life, but instead of gathering courage, trusting God, and walking tall in your call, you saw yourself as incapable or too small to proceed? Not only that, but perhaps you thought others saw you as feeble and unqualified as well.

If you were sitting down with Moses, he would know exactly what you were talking about. Deuteronomy 1:8 was written about fourteen hundred years before Christ came and was one of Moses' final messages to the children of Israel: "See, I have set the land before you; go in and possess the land, which the LORD swore to your fathers—to Abraham, Isaac, and Jacob" (NKJV). This sounds like a great message, but here's where everything went wrong. All the leaders started talking to Moses and told him that going into the Promised Land was a risky thing. They got fearful.

The next decision Moses made cost him dearly. He was never permitted by God to enter into the new land. Instead of doing as God had said and simply walk into the destiny and promise laid before him, he formed a committee and took votes on whether they should trust God or move forward in their own wisdom on the matter. As you may remember, they sent out twelve spies and only two came back with a positive report, even though God had promised the land to them.

The other ten said the fruit of the land was abundant and the land was flowing with milk and honey, but the enemy was too powerful for them to overcome. They saw the giants living in the land and said in Numbers 13:33, "… we were like grasshoppers in our own sight, and so we were in their sight" (NKJV). What's interesting is not only did they see *themselves* as small insects, but they said the *enemy* saw them as grasshoppers, too. But the enemy hadn't even spotted them or they would have been chased down and killed. So they *imagined* in their own minds that the enemy saw them as tiny, weak bugs. We sometimes believe what we think are other people's perceived perspectives on our being, rather than believing we are who God says we are!

Moses reminded the people of all the miracles God had done for them as they went through the wilderness. He told them there was no need to worry, but they would not hear it and their hearts were gripped with fear. Their unbelief grieved the Lord. Instead of believing God, they looked at things from their human perspective through the lens of their own reason.

What is even more thought provoking is the fact that after Moses died, when Joshua was leading the people, he again sent spies to scout out the city of Jericho which God had promised to give to the Children of Israel. When the spies came under cover of night to the prostitute Rahab's house, she declared in Joshua 2:9-11, "I know that the LORD has given you the land, that the terror of you has fallen on us, and that all the inhabitants of the land are fainthearted because of you. For we have heard how the LORD dried up the water of the Red Sea for you when you came out of Egypt, and what you did to the two kings of the Amorites who were on the other side of the Jordan, Sihon and Og, whom you utterly destroyed. And as soon as we heard these things, our hearts melted; neither did there remain any more courage in anyone because of you, for the LORD your God, He is God in heaven above and on earth beneath" (NKJV).

Do you see the utter craziness of this situation? The Israelites cowered in fear because they saw themselves as grasshoppers all those years, when in fact *their enemies* were melting in fear because of the stories they heard about how God had delivered Israel time and time again. To this day, our enemy knows even more than we do about how powerful God is and the terror of you has fallen on him. In fact, he is faint-hearted because of you. We cannot afford to underestimate the power of Almighty God in our lives. I pray the terror of us, empowered by our Relentless Redeemer will fall on the enemy every single day we wake up in the authority of the Blood of Christ. May he become faint-hearted because of us. We are terrifying to him when we understand what God can do through us!

God may birth a dream in our hearts for a great work that He is going to accomplish, but instead of rising up in faith when we see a giant in front of us, we see ourselves as grasshoppers—small and inept. If God paved the way to your Promised Land, run, don't walk to take it! Release your fears to God and pursue all He has laid before you. There are dreams in your heart ready for you to lay hold of. Trust God and see Him work powerfully on your behalf to bring about your greatest destiny.

I was in danger of completely giving up on everything God had for me. I had received so many negative responses that I thought I was crazy to keep pursuing the call in my heart. I truly felt I had not completed what God had put in my heart to do back on my living room floor in 1999. He asked me to tell people about Jesus on television and I hadn't really done that. *Did I miss the boat?* I was so confused.

The only thing in media that had any kind of positive note to it was from my good friend, Andrew Westlund. He and his amazing wife, Phebe, had started a company back in the day when no one had a cell phone. The first generation phones were clunky and expensive so most people could not afford them and they did not fit nicely in a purse.

Andrew, being an incredible visionary, had this idea that maybe ... just maybe ... one day everyone would own a cell phone. However, not everyone agreed with him. He and Phebe took every dime they had and risked it all to pursue their dream by opening up the very first retail cell phone store in downtown Vancouver. It was a huge leap of faith!

Andrew knew that I was out of work so he asked me to come and produce some video segments for his company. I turned him down a couple of times because my passion was not to produce corporate videos. But Andrew would not take no for an answer. I gave him a high hourly rate, thinking he would withdraw his request, but he simply said, "Great, when can you start?"

Ironically, Andrew's current success and ability to appreciate others had come from a lesson he had learned many years earlier. He told me in his quest to be significant, first with his parents, then with high school friends, and later with those in business, it finally dawned on him one day that nobody really cared. While this might seem like a devastating realization, to Andrew it was actually the beginning of his attainment.

He had tried so hard to please everyone but in the end, no one truly acknowledged his efforts or noticed his strides. He subsequently considered that whatever happened in life, he would first and foremost have to be able to live with the consequences of his actions himself. He stopped trying to win the approval of everyone else and simply lived his life to the fullest, ignoring the naysayers and dissenters.

At this same time, Maralee Dawn was also an encouraging friend. She did a children's television series that was seen in almost every country in the world. On top of that, she produced an inspiring series of interviews that told incredible stories of women across the globe. One day she called and asked if I wanted to go to a media conference in Atlanta, Georgia, with her. I told her I wasn't in the media so I couldn't possibly use my family's finances to pay for a trip to pursue a dream that God seemed to be shutting down.

She plainly and succinctly said, "You are supposed to be on television!" I had to smile at her faith. She told me to call Andrew to see if he would send me to promote his new business series idea. It seemed like a real long shot for Andrew to send me, but I said I would ask him anyway. Before calling him, I said a quick prayer.

Andrew immediately said he would send me on his air miles. It was a done deal within minutes—just like that I was going to Atlanta, Georgia, to the International Christian Visual Media (ICVM) Conference and I wasn't even in the media. Isaiah 65:24 (GNT) says, "Even before they finish praying to me, I will answer their prayers."

Andrew's unique perspective on business was something I really believed in and thought might open some doors for him to have a show. Suddenly, a very strange turn of events was about to shock my life and bring about the most sweeping days of vindication that I had ever experienced. It was far more than I could ever have imagined or dreamed. The Word of God is true. Philippians 1:6 says, "Being confident of this very thing, that he which hath begun a good work in you will perform it until the day of Jesus Christ" (KJV).

I could not have guessed what lay just ahead but I knew I had learned the secret of abiding in God. The greatest key to joy, peace, contentment, and security is through simply *being* in Him. When stress comes, I now release it so I can abide, inhabit, dwell, and simply be in Him. When I feel insecure, I remember that I abide in the safety of a God who accepts me unconditionally.

When I am discouraged, I look to the Vine, from whom I gain life and vitality. The Vine steadfastly, unwaveringly, ceaselessly holds me where I cannot be dislodged or removed. I abide—though weak, broken, marred, confused, in pain, or rejected by others. I simply abide. "I am the vine, you are the branches. He who abides in Me, and I in him, bears much fruit; for without Me you can do nothing. If anyone does not abide in Me, he is cast out as a branch and is withered; and they gather them and throw them into the fire, and they are burned. If you abide in Me, and My words abide in you, you will ask what you desire, and it shall be done for you" (John 15:5-7, NKJV).

Is there really any way to explain how the circumstances of life come to be? Ecclesiastes 9:11 says, "The race is not to the swift, nor the battle to the strong, nor bread to the wise, nor riches to men of understanding, nor favor to men of skill; but time and chance happen to them all" (NKJV). Proverbs 16:9 declares, "A man's mind plans his way, but the Lord directs his steps and makes them sure."

Maralee Dawn and I had a wonderful time in Atlanta and she was kind enough to introduce me to many of her long-time production and television contacts—people from across the globe who were passionate about producing all kinds of media that glorified God. I was able to present to many of them the concept of Andrew's reality business show, depicting spiritual principles in a secular business environment.

As I was making my way through the crowd on the final afternoon, suddenly Maralee burst into my path with a very excited and yet serious look on her face. She said that she was going to introduce me to some very important people. She explained that I was about to meet two very noteworthy people: an executive producer and a programming director for a very large broadcaster in Canada.

Tore (pronounced Tora), was a very savvy dresser, not afraid to wear a pink shirt under his dark suit. He looked smart and stern. He was not overly friendly and I detected a slight accent from his Norwegian roots. The next five minutes found me stumbling over my words, which I noticed made Maralee fidget and blink a lot. I somehow mentioned, for no other reason than to mock myself, that I had a treatment for a program where a professional football player and I would host a show. I further light-heartedly stated I had been told it would never work, so I had pretty much shelved the idea. I casually went on to explain that the football player was an African-American guy, but that I was really more African-American than him, because I was actually born in Africa. I laughed at my own joke. Tore just stared at me. I will never forget, however, a barely noticeable look of interest that crossed his face.

He asked me if I would do a pilot for the show. *I guess so,* I thought. The meeting in the hallway ended as quickly as it had started and it was then that I noticed I had a run in my pantyhose. I was clueless that the conversation of those last five minutes was going to change my life. I enjoyed the rest of the trip and flew home.

# 13

# THE DREAM LIVES

*He shall come as a Redeemer to Zion and to those in Jacob (Israel)*
*who turn from transgression, says the Lord.*

**- Isaiah 59:20**

Zack and I had come to the end of our forty-day epic battle in court. Truth was revealed again and again during the proceedings. It was one of the scariest projects I have ever undertaken, yet I came away with strength of character to endure and overcome. In his final decision, the judge made a wise and fair analysis of our case and I grew to have a profound respect for the wisdom of the judiciary. I'm sure many judges make mistakes and not everyone is happy with their decisions, but in our case, Justice Brine was the best.

Zack had a new woman in his life and she really helped to smooth the waters for a season until their relationship ended. I chose to forgive all the harsh words and accusations leveled in the courtroom. It had been a fight for all we were worth, financially, physically and emotionally. I continued to ask God to help me forgive the difficulties I felt Zack brought into my life. As He did, we began to speak to one another in a kinder way. I prayed blessing into his life and began to speak words of encouragement towards him.

It's interesting to me now that when God eventually brings us to the conclusion of a wilderness experience, we may not even recognize the signs. It's a good thing that through it all, we become content to rest in God and stop striving to make things happen on our own. Hopefully, we have matured to the place where we leave everything in His hands, allowing events to come about at His appointed time. Nonetheless, we may forget for a short while that God is a miracle working God—but when He steps in, it is going to be a real show!

A man by the name of Yves Perriard has written an essay entitled, "Four Phases of the Wilderness." I found his entire essay on this subject to be a brilliant summary of the journey we all take at some point, probably three or four times in our lifetime, according to my 83-year-old friend Greta Sheppard. Perriard wrote the following about the end of the wilderness experience:

*At the beginning of this final stage, God usually gives us some signs in advance that our situation will end, in order to encourage us. It can be a supernatural revelation, a dream or an intuition that shows us that things will take a different turn, or it can be through people or conditions that give us a clear confirmation of what is already in our hearts. Usually, if we have fully surrendered and not put false hopes in people or circumstances (as we used to do in the early stages of our desert times), then we can recognize God's voice for ourselves. It is very important in this final phase that we keep on with the same attitude of trust and peace that we had in the third stage, by not forcing out the final outcome. Often, when we see the light at the end of the tunnel, we can be tempted to speed up the final process, instead of having the patience to wait on God. He has the perfect timing, and sometimes this final stage of the whole process may take longer than we hoped.*

*The reason we do not have to speed things up is that the desert times usually finish with a dramatic turn-around. After 14 years, the slave Joseph becomes prime minister overnight. After 40 years, the long forgotten Moses suddenly comes back and within days, two nations are completely shaken. After 3-4 years, Elijah radically revolutionizes everything in one day at Mt. Carmel. After 30 years, Jesus, who is not known before, ends his desert experience and starts his ministry with a spectacular demonstration of miraculous power. God may keep us a long time in the waiting, but when He moves, it is fast and with power![3]*

Personally, I had no idea that my dramatic turn-around was coming. Maybe I'm just like the elephant that's tied to a tree and when the rope is removed, it still doesn't leave the area. I had become so accustomed to being spurned that I actually did not recognize an open door.

I came back home from the ICVM in Atlanta with no thought to pursue Tore's request for a pilot show. I went about my daily business and once in awhile a memory would come to remind me of his request, but in my heart, I thought it would be a big waste of time and money

---

[3] Yves Perriard. "Four Phases of the Wilderness." *The Ellis County Press*, January 15, 2011. http://www.elliscountypress.com/inspirational/10999-four-phases-of-the-wilderness.html

to produce a pilot. Nothing would come of it anyway, and frankly, I was just fine with how my life was turning out working with the youth.

What I found in my own wilderness was that God changed my identity. Prior to a desert experience, we place our sense of security in a position, an act of service, a place of honor, our wealth, family, talents or abilities. But God wants us to find ourselves so secure in Him that nothing rattles us—even when we experience great loss.

About two months later, I ran into Mark Washington at the grocery store. I was thrilled to see him again and after asking about his beautiful wife Judy and their children, I quickly told him I talked about the show idea in Atlanta. "They asked me to do a pilot." Mark looked at me and lifted one of his eyebrows like he does and said, "Well shouldn't we be doing one then?"

*Shouldn't we be doing one then?* That question rang in my mind the rest of the day. I went home and talked it over with JT. Only then did I think that since JT works at a studio, he would be able to rent it to shoot the pilot. *Why hadn't this occurred to me sooner?* He said he would check into it and within a couple of days, he had a very reasonable quote from the studio to book it for a day—including all the necessary crew. The cost was far less than I thought it would be.

Suddenly I had a desire to get the pilot done; it was burning in my heart. I called Mark and we arranged for a time to shoot the pilot. Within two weeks, I booked the guests, crew and studio. I also produced the rundowns. We were ready to go!

It was so fun to be back in the studio again. Ironically, we shot the pilot on the set of *Urban Rush*—the first show I had volunteered to do graphics for. God brought me full circle, back to the very place He had birthed the dream. I was now sitting in the exact spot I had once dared to believe God would take me. Something ignited in my heart that day! When we do by faith what God puts in our heart, He will anoint the work and bring about a miracle, one step at a time. We do the *possible* and God does the *impossible!*

On October 14, 2007, I had not yet sent the pilot to Tore. It was in the process of being edited. I wrote in my journal the words of TD Jakes, "I think my mistakes made my miracles ... my misery made my ministry." I also wrote a page entitled, "What Has God Been Saying to Me" with ten things I felt He spoke to my heart that day.

1. *Rest in Me.*

2. *I have destined you to do a great work. I will bring it to pass.*

3. *You're going to have a national presence in the media.*

4. *Worship, don't worry.*

5. *I'm bigger than any problems.*

6. *I'll take your mess and make it your message.*

7. *My Word, engrafted into your heart, will heal, restore and promote you.*

8. *You need to understand who you are and what I have created you to be – get a sense of entitlement!*

9. *The Word works, so teach it and preach it.*

10. *God is going to give you a new confidence in the talents He has for you. You need to see that I have equipped you with all that you need to do the job.*

The pilot was edited together and we added some simple music and graphics, then sent it off to Tore. I called Tore to let him know I had forwarded it to him. When he received it on Monday, November 5, 2007, he sent me a one-sentence email. "I got the pilot; will be in touch." I assumed he would watch it later that day and I would hear back from him shortly. However, when Tuesday, Wednesday and Thursday came and went, I had a sinking feeling that he wasn't interested and God was going to close the door once again.

I had an entry in my diary on November 11th, wherein I recounted the events of the previous week. The lupus in my body had gotten worse than ever and I was in a lot of pain. Zack sent a scathing letter about me to the school and called the police to report me for writing letters to him about the children. Thankfully it was not against the law for one parent to write the other concerning their children. It seemed as though all hell was breaking loose against me. I wrote, "I feel alone and solemn." I felt the pilot was going nowhere and perhaps it was not God's time for me to have a show. *And then I prayed...*

On Friday morning, I woke up with a desperate prayer on my heart.

*God, help me to accept Your will and not my own. I've had such high hopes for doing television again and nothing has worked out.*

*I have had no calls acknowledging any opportunities. I surrender my will and my desires. If You want me to look after high-risk youth for the rest of my life, I will do it. I love You and I know You love me and have redeemed me from so much. Whatever You want me to do, I will do, amen.*

*AND ONE FINAL THING, LORD, I know Who You are. I know that You are the Master of the universe and with one word from Your mouth, You can change my life forever. The Word says we have not because we ask not. So I am asking You today for the miraculous. I pray by the power and in the name of Jesus You would open doors no man can shut. I ask You for divine favor so astounding it will be clearly known it is You who has brought it about. I am praying for the dynamic, unstoppable power of God to directly intervene in my situation and open the way for a show to begin. You are God and I know what You can do. I release my life into Your hands. I will spend the rest of my life doing Your will. Jesus, I am Yours and Yours alone.*

I felt absolutely nothing as I prayed this, but then faith welled up in my heart as I spoke those words. I had no reason to believe in the natural that God would do anything. I said the words by sheer will and determination. One might say I had no faith, but as I look back, I had tremendous faith in what God could do in spite of my feelings. Hebrews 11:1, 3 and 6 says, "Now faith is the substance of things hoped for, the evidence of things not seen. By faith we understand the universe was formed at God's command, so that what is seen was not made out of what was visible. And without faith it is impossible to please God, because anyone who comes to Him must believe that He exists and that He rewards those who earnestly seek Him" (NIV84).

At the very moment I was praying, across the country, a meeting was about to take place with Tore and his business associate, Todd, which would have huge ramifications in my life. When God profoundly begins to reveal the surprises He has been preparing, held in secret until the appointed time, it is a momentous and stunning day. 1 Corinthians 2:9 says, "However, as it is written: "What no eye has seen, what no ear has heard, and what no human mind has conceived" — the things God has prepared for those who love him—" (NIV).

That afternoon I went to pick up my high-risk youth from their school at 2:00 p.m. They were involved in an altercation at school and were continuing their disagreement in the car. I was trying to help them reasonably work it out and also mentioned I didn't appreciate the older one, Malcolm, peeing on the fence. He started giggling and explained he was from a farm in the interior of British Columbia and no one had ever gotten upset at him for peeing on a fence. He said he didn't actually know it would bother me. He promised never to do it again, offering me a high-five.

I slapped his hand, rolled my eyes and sighed heavily. How could I be angry at this kid? There was so much to love about his crazy ways. He had been abandoned by his mom, had no idea where his dad was and felt like an outcast. He had become involved with a group of street friends who were nothing but trouble and they led him to commit a home invasion in which he put kids in the closet. He said he still felt sick about it.

The cause of the altercation was our other youth had stolen a small item from our office and Malcolm had become enraged that he would dare to steal 'from the hands that fed us.' He forced the other kid, who never knew Malcolm had told us about the theft, to return the item to our office or else he was going to beat the living stuffing out of him. It was funny to see how Malcolm had become so attached to us. He actually called us a couple years later to say thank you for all we had done for him.

Suddenly on this regular afternoon, my cell phone rang. I blindly reached over the console and down into my purse, feeling around until I found my phone. I looked at the display and saw that it was Tore. I took a deep breath and braced myself. *Remember Laura-Lynn, God loves you. If God is for you, who can be against you? It's okay if Tore hates the pilot; you're not a loser.* Tore started by saying that I had probably heard the news that the network he worked for had just purchased Channel 10 (the station I had been fired from). I had not heard that.

He said they had been in a meeting that morning with the programming executives. The meeting got started late and while they waited, his business associate, Todd, had a look at the pilot. During the meeting, Tore and Todd presented Mark Washington and me as the possible hosts for a show concept the network wanted to do in our area. The executives thought this could work well and gave the go-ahead to Tore to proceed with determining the viability. Tore said they needed to know how serious Mark and I were about doing a daily show—256 episodes a year.

"We're serious, Tore, very serious!" I tried to act casual and professional, not betraying that my insides were jumping up and down, doing cartwheels across the floorboards of my mind. I didn't want to seem too eager. Tore said they were flying out to our area in three days and asked if Mark and I could meet them at the Pan Pacific Hotel. After we agreed to do this, I hung up and stood there for a moment trying to comprehend the conversation I just had. *Is this for real? Am I dreaming or having a hallucination?* I bit my hand to see if it hurt. I started laughing out loud; this could not be happening!

On this day, at this moment, it was as if the dead place inside of me came to life again. Something rose within me that had not dared to breathe for a long time. God knew all along what would happen, but He never let me in on this surprise. I didn't have the words to express how I felt. I was in a daze as I walked into the house. I asked Malcolm to stop pretending to be Batman as he jumped off the couch. Then I stopped, looking right at him and smiling from ear to ear, "Oh, who cares Malcolm. Pretend to be anything you want." I flopped onto the couch, "It might actually come true one day!" I laughed again.

I almost let my dreams die in the wilderness, but let's face it, great men and women of God have done the same thing. Moses murdered an Egyptian and then wandered in the desert for 40 years. *I wonder if he let his dream die out there?* Joseph had a dream that his brothers would bow to him, instead they sold him into slavery and through a false accusation, he ended up in prison. *I wonder if his dreams died in that jail cell?* Ruth married Naomi's son and then he passed away. She was left a widow, along with her mother-in-law, and moved to Judah where she didn't know anyone. She was alone. *Did her dreams to be loved die in that desperate circumstance?*

Mary and Martha sent word to Jesus to come quickly so He could heal their beloved brother Lazarus. But Jesus took His time getting there and Lazarus died. *Was their mourning and anger at Jesus a sign they had lost their hope?* I guarantee you, they could not have dreamed of what Jesus was about to do next. Not only was He going to raise Lazarus from the dead, but quite possibly more significantly, He was going to raise their dreams from the dead.

One moment with Jesus will bring your dreams back to life again. One miraculous encounter with God will remind you that the gift within you is irrevocable and it is time to let it rise again. Have your dreams died? Have you forgotten who Jesus is? One word from His lips and you can walk on water. We can limit our future to our own reduced thinking—forgetting we were born for great purpose and that destiny resides within us. It's easy to forget we were crafted by the Master to do damage to the enemy's kingdom. We are unstoppable when we are attached to the Source of all power!

As I look back, I can see the deliberate hand of God opening every door, while closing many. I remember asking why He would shut the very doors I thought would be the key to unlocking my destiny. I could not understand why He left me in darkness crying out to Him. I wondered if He had forgotten me, or even worse, what if He didn't care? All I could do was surrender. There was little choice. Ironically, in that surrender He saw the very heart and attitude He could finally use.

I had not correctly discerned nor understood the Word, which says in 2 Corinthians 13:4 (NKJV), "For though He was crucified in weakness, yet He lives by the power of God. For we also are weak in Him, but we shall live with Him by the power of God toward you." On certain unexpected days, a swift twist of divine fate would reveal redemption, restoration, and a vindication so magnificent that it could only be God's hand of power. A piece of the puzzle would be strategically placed, unveiling a masterpiece. In a season in which I had submitted to a lower place than I had hoped for, supernatural occurrences revealed that all along, He was creating a spacious place for my destiny to reign far greater than I could have imagined or dreamed.

It's a mystery that our plight, at times, seems grievous and hard and yet within this very adversity is born the character that must be present for us to walk down providential roads of destiny. God always knew what and who you would become. He simply had to get you ready to hold the weight of glory He longed to bestow upon you. Romans 11:2 says, "No, God has not rejected and disowned His people [whose destiny] He had marked out and appointed and foreknown from the beginning." If it appears today that God has forgotten you, relinquish your hopes, dreams and fears to Him in surrender—trust Him with every detail. Until He sees this posture, He cannot trust you with the enormity of the call that resides within you.

The next few days were euphoric. I couldn't think of much else except this incredible new development. There was not an ounce of sadness or pain left, or any questions about why God had allowed me to lose my job or had been so silent. The mystery that had confounded me for a year and a half was coming together and the picture being created was inconceivable.

I called Mark and we met with Tore and Todd on November 12, 2007. Todd had an extraordinary way of presenting the gospel in a truly unique manner. Tore and Todd wanted to know if Mark and I were completely committed to the process and hard work of hosting a daily show. We just kept nodding our heads indicating that yes, we were very ready.

In a staggering, completely unexpected, sweeping moment of redemption, vindication and restoration, I was back on the air. I didn't realize that the program I was fired from would be cancelled and replaced by the new show, *The Daily with Mark and Laura-Lynn*. The new show held the same time slot and aired on the same local channel that I was fired from. This was astounding!

Someone who saw Don, my former producer, the day this news was announced, told me his face went ashen gray. He would have no say over my life, my calling or my journey, but I already knew that he never did. God needed me to leave the station so that a larger, more spacious place could be prepared for me. Psalm 31:8 states, "You have not given me into the hands of the enemy, but have set my feet in a spacious place" (NIV). This entire experience taught me lessons that will remain with me for the rest of my life. If we seek Him, we will find Him. Psalm 118:5 says, "When hard pressed, I cried to the LORD; he brought me into a spacious place." A spacious place, a place of destiny, provision and influence had indeed opened before my eyes and I knew I had nothing to do with it.

The furor in the next few weeks was intense. Todd flew in several times to negotiate studio rental and to get us prepared for the mammoth job ahead. I heard that some folks at the station were angry with me and felt I had somehow manipulated people and circumstances in order to get a show on their station. I had to laugh. I'm just not that brilliant! I would be proud to take more credit, but there's no way I could.

I put out a peace offering to Don at one point by sending him a note asking to bury the hatchet. He never responded—but that's okay. I'm grateful today that he did what he did. Jack issued a station-wide memo congratulating their "former colleague, Laura-Lynn," on the new show and said some very nice things. It was a jaw-dropping season. Jack also apologized to me and said they made a big mistake in letting me go. I told him that everything was as it was supposed to have been. God is in control, not man.

God orchestrated all of the events. It cost me my ego, pride, self-will and stubbornness. But it was well worth the price. My life was hidden with Christ in God and my identity had found its rightful place. The accusations and complaints from some of those at the station unfortunately continued well into the production of *The Daily* and I was sometimes surprised and other times hurt. I found comfort in the Word of God. Psalm 31:20 says, "In the shelter of your presence you hide them from all human intrigues; you keep them safe in your dwelling from accusing tongues" (NIV).

I had more fun than a barrel of monkeys for the next year and a half, as Mark and I shared our hearts, lives and laughter with the audience. I thought I even heard God laugh. I had a clothing sponsor who provided me with 20 different outfits per monthly shoot, hair and make-up artists who made me shine, a production crew that was wonderful to work with, and producers who took care of the details so I could just do what God called me to do. My heart was filled with joy and I often pinched myself to see if it was all truly real.

I had the opportunity to interview Ted McGinley of *Hope and Faith* and dozens of other well-known celebrities. I met one of my dearest friends to this day, Dr. Susan Biali, author of *Live a Life You Love - 7 Steps to a Healthier, Happier, More Passionate You.* She gave us fascinating information on health and wellness throughout the tenure of the show. Her journey through her own wilderness in search of her identity is extraordinary. She has the gifted, brilliant mind of a doctor and yet, she simply wanted to be a dancer. Her authenticity has now brought her to a spacious place of influence that sets people free to pursue their path of destiny.

As is so often the case though, all good things must come to an end. The large network that owned Channel 10 was sold and new management took over. Our show contract was not renewed and we wound up our tapings with a sad goodbye. Todd and Tore threw a cast party to celebrate what had been an incredible experience. It was the end of the most fun I had ever had doing television, but I still had not yet been able to freely tell people about Jesus on television. That call still rang very clearly in my heart.

The sadness over the show ending didn't linger long, however, nor did I feel any pain or rejection. I love getting older because I get wiser.

There was nothing to indicate I would ever do television again, but there was this peace over my being that my identity was not in question because of this loss. I had grown to love the media and its ability to communicate love, joy, laughter and peace. I realized that it gave me the opportunity to enter thousands of homes, invited of course, and share my life with people with one click of their remote. People would meet me on the street and say they felt like they knew me. It was beautiful; it always made me smile.

Life returned to a normal pace. Tore left his production equipment in the area for a while and I found several ways to put it to good use. I paid for the camera crews myself to film interviews with Liz Curtis Higgs, Tammy Trent and Josh McDowell. I was the first person with whom Josh shared his very personal story on camera of being sexually abused as a child. It was an incredible testimony on the power of forgiveness.

I got up on Sunday, May 11, 2009, with a little ache in my stomach. I had been in thoughtful discourse with God for a few days. I had questions about my future and what I was supposed to do. I knew I could make things happen but wondered if I should simply submit and let life bring me to where I was meant to be in God's time. There is a very big difference in these two positions. One is based in a place when you are driven by ego to accomplish—the other is based in a place of surrender to the destiny you were born to live. One is driven by fear—the other by faith.

I was at a party and met Thomas McClary, the founder and original guitarist for the Commodores. He discovered Lionel Richie. I remembered this man well from a time I had interviewed him for *The Daily*. What I recalled about him was the supernatural soul power that emanated from him as he spoke.

I asked him if we could interview him again and he agreed. We set the interview up for a couple days later. The shoot went well. I loved hearing his heart and his stories of the early days of the Commodores and how God's thumbprint had been on it. At the end of our shoot, I drove him and his wife back to their hotel. On my drive home, I told the Lord my heart's desire was to make television that would inspire people to be closer to Him.

I reminisced about all the great men and women of faith that I had been blessed to interview over the last few years such as Tony Campolo, Dr. Gary Smalley, Pastor Bill Hybels, the incredible Patsy Clairmont, Dr. Gary Chapman and Billy Graham's daughter, Gigi. It was intriguing to hear their personal stories and it always felt like I gleaned just a touch of their spirit during the interview.

That summer I attended an amazing event in Nashville called the NRB (National Religious Broadcasters). I met a woman named Suellen Roberts, the founder and president of Christian Women in Media. She had a gathering where I was able to meet outstanding women like Joni Erickson Tada and Kay Arthur. These women are mentors in the faith to me. Another great lady who shared her heart and passion for writing was author and speaker, Karol Kinder Ladd. She offered a short class on how to step out and write the book that God has put on your heart. The things she shared that day are the seeds that have enabled me to write this book.

Karol took a picture of me with Dr. James Dobson, who was having lunch in the same restaurant. Thinking back, it's embarrassing what comes over me. I felt I just had to meet Dr. Dobson because I had listened to his broadcasts most of my life. I went over to ask to have my picture taken with him and somehow, we had to actually move his whole table in order to accommodate my request. The two men he was with graciously got out of the way and I told Dr. Dobson I was shaking because I was so glad to meet him. "Oh for goodness sakes!" he laughed. He was my hero! When I got home, it was really distressing to realize that in the picture, the fly on my slacks was down the whole time!

My heart began to be burdened to go back to Uganda. God had placed this vision in my heart to go, but I did not have a traveling companion. Ruth Moody, my extraordinary friend whose husband had recently passed away, heard I was returning for the 50th year anniversary of the work in Kampala started by Hugh and Audrey Layzell, who had dedicated me as a baby. Ruth offered to travel with me and then blessed me beyond measure by completely covering my fare! I was thrilled that she would come with me on this adventure.

I wanted to do a project in Uganda that would impact someone there, but I found myself at a complete loss of what to do. I almost gave up on the idea, except for the fact that Ruth had made this astounding offer to pay for the first class flight all the way to Africa! I could not possibly give up after she had made such a generous contribution.

In late 2009, I met the vice president of Uganda in Vancouver. His personal assistant was a wonderful Christian man named

Joseph Lukwago, who later became a dear friend. I called Joseph and he informed me of a desperate woman named Maria. Her land had been passed down from generation to generation but her home was a deplorable mud hut. She lived with her three grandchildren since her daughter had died of AIDS.

I threw a fundraiser for Maria before my trip to Uganda, using sheer guts and determination. This was a tremendous stretch for me, because I don't typically organize things like this. It took everything I had to pull it off, but we raised the funds for a new home for Maria in one evening. The Vice President's builders built her a beautiful new brick home with a water tank, gutters and a solar lighting panel.

When I arrived with Ruth in Uganda, we went to see Maria and dedicated her new home to the Lord. Her personality was stunning as she embraced us and bowed to the ground in thankfulness for what had been done. She had had the worst house in the area—rivers of water engulfed her flea-infested home when it rained. Now she had a lovely brick home.

Maria was well-known in the community for her beautiful spirit, but her plight was very sad. Ruth and I stood amazed as we heard one man say that from the moment Maria knew she was going to have a new home, she began to have the countenance and strength of a younger woman. One of the vice president's men told me that because of Maria's miraculous provision, he truly believed there was a God.

Maria praised God that He saw her in the despondency of her circumstances. I could not believe how the majestic hand of the Father moved on behalf of one lone, poor, grandmother in a remote village of Africa. God had ensured that one blonde girl born in Uganda and a widow from Canada would feel so moved that they would invest themselves in a woman they did not know, but whom God had seen and had compassion for. In one awe-inspiring transaction, God turned Maria's world upside down, as only He can do. Relentless redemption pursued the most marginalized and forgotten of all humanity and dispersed a staggering resolution to her trouble.

I came home in wonderment of God's love for the very least of us. I was so grateful that Ruth and I were used as the hands of Jesus to touch Maria's precious life. Ruth and her family later provided the funds for a home for another beautiful family in Uganda. So far four homes have been built through generous donations.

Eventually all of the camera and production equipment was shipped back to Ontario so I couldn't do any more interviews. I wondered if that was it; was all the television fun over? Still, there was a knowing in my "knower" that it wasn't over. I couldn't see any doors opening but I had been here before and had seen God do miraculous things. My heart rested and trusted that God was in control and His will would reign in my life. True enough, behind the scenes in rooms I was not privy to and through negotiations I knew nothing of, God was working to bring about another glorious chapter in my life.

In the meantime, I was still working with the street youth. One exceptional young girl who was put in our home was Jasmine. *And did she ever keep me busy!* She was 14 years old and angry at the world. She had gotten addicted to crack cocaine and would run away to prostitute the moment we had our backs turned. She ran away twice and I tracked her down in a very rough neighborhood because I prayed and asked God where she was.

The first time, she was in a parking lot behind a fast food joint. She was sitting there with a woman who was known in the area to police as one of the prime recruiters into prostitution. I opened my car door and stood on the lip of the vehicle, "Get in the car Jasmine! And YOU," I said, pointing at the woman, "you leave her alone! She is 14 years old and you have no business trying to destroy her life!" To my surprise, Jasmine scooted up and hopped in my car obediently. That was not expected. For all I knew, I would have to wrestle her to the ground. The older prostitute stared me down and began sauntering away with an arrogant swagger, giving me the finger. With Jasmine now safely in my vehicle, I rolled down the window, lifted my sunglasses off my head and told the woman on the street, "If you ever speak to her again, you are going to become my problem! Do you hear me?"

She turned around and with eyes colder than ice she said, "You better take better care of her then!" *Well that just infuriated me!* I had worked constantly to keep Jasmine from running away but this time she had escaped from one of her youth workers. "I'm warning you!" I yelled out the window. I drove away and the older prostitute gave me an inappropriate gesture again. Jasmine looked in shock as she stared straight ahead.

"You're lucky you're not dead," she said with surprise in her voice. "I've seen that woman beat the ---- out of people in a back alley."

"Well," I retorted, "I am not afraid of her and if I find you down here again, we are all gonna regret it!" The next time I went looking for Jasmine, I was with another former youth, Colleen, who liked to hang out with our family and was extremely talkative. She insisted that I pray for Mr. Bundy and Stan, her guinea pigs, to not be lonely that night as she was out late. "I am not praying for your dumb guinea pigs! We have to find Jasmine!"

"I thought you said to pray about everything?" Colleen was more than annoyed that I didn't think this was important enough to pray about.

"Oh fine! Dear God, please help Mr. Bundy and Stan to be at peace tonight as Colleen is not yet home with them and help Mr. Bundy with his bladder issue." I prayed in exasperation, "ALSO, more importantly, could you please help us find Jasmine."

Jasmine had been missing for about five hours and I couldn't sleep unless I personally drove around looking for her, even though the police had already been notified. We drove around for about twenty minutes, as I kept praying out loud, "Please God, where is she?" We came to a four-way stop and Colleen said to turn right as she mentioned she had found one of her fake nails in the dishwasher. I felt I needed to go left.

We drove about two more blocks and there, sitting on the curb, again with another woman from the streets, was Jasmine. A rush of relief swept over me. I leaned out the window and let the woman know that Jasmine was 14 and she shouldn't be out here. The woman looked at Jasmine and confronted her because she had told her that she was 21; Jasmine did look much older than 14. "Get in the car Jasmine," I motioned to her. Sulking and angry, Jasmine got in the car and slammed the door. "How did you know where I was?" she scowled.

"God told me," I said slowly, raising one eyebrow and casting a stern glance toward the back seat.

Jasmine was the toughest youth we ever had, but when she was upset, she asked me to read the Bible to her and pray. We sat on the floor and she always held my hands. She rocked back and forth as I prayed and would say, "Yes, Jesus, yes Jesus. Please make my life better and help me to go back home."

She has long since gone home but she still calls once in a while to laugh and remember what we call "the good old days." She remembers going to camp and giving her heart to Jesus. "I love you," she always says as we hang up.

While writing this book, I have had the incredible opportunity to ponder my miraculous journey. We all have a story and yours will bear great similarity to mine, not in the specific details, but in the ways and means God chooses to prepare your vessel for great use. The Apostle Paul wrote in 2 Corinthians 12:10, "That is why, for Christ's sake, I delight in weaknesses, in insults, in hardships, in persecutions, in difficulties. For when I am weak, then I am strong" (NIV). There comes a day when God tests you through the fire of adversity and chisels your character so forcefully that you are finally a vessel prepared for extraordinary use.

You might think that the dark, debilitating processes you have experienced means you are out of the race. The wounding, pruning and pounding of your limp clay spirit as He molded and shaped you, while grinding out the impurities, may have seemed almost impossible to bear at times. You may have wondered if God is so cruel that He would break your will and pride so completely that there would be nothing left of you. The nights have been long and the days left you wasting away with no vindication and no exoneration in sight.

You may have cried out to God and only heard an echo of your own voice, as if there was no one listening at all. With nothing but sheer hope and faith in Jesus that He could hear you in the silence, you may have surrendered to being content to eat the crumbs from under the table. Your own weaknesses, failures and humanity may seem to have left you with nothing but an empty shell. Perhaps you have resigned yourself to a lower position than you once dreamed. But as you release your quest for power and a title, you will find the peace that passes all understanding.

As God surely hovered silently over His child, He saw the budding of a beautiful creation—one with a priceless value, noble worth and fit for great use. He had been waiting for these signs of submission and that unmistakable crack of the breaking away of all self-will. With a thunderous cry through the heavens, "It is time!" our Father picks us up and with an obvious gleam in His eye, places us in a position of great purpose for the Kingdom. To our amazement, it is a far greater place than we had originally dreamed—beyond all we could have asked or thought. The fire has done its work and our fabric has been woven into the strength of granite. Who knew all this breaking would one day lead to your ultimate making?

Some of you are living in relentless redemption—where the seeming brutality of life has paved the way for your greatest destiny. Now you can see that God never let you go. Looking at the ground-up pieces of your own will, you now relinquish your self-importance to a far greater, wiser, and more powerful place of complete reliance on Christ. Others may still be in the heat of the firing kiln…don't worry, everything is going to be all right. God has a great plan for your life. All you need to do is surrender. Never give up. Your greatest days are just ahead!

I kept in touch with Tore and would shoot some ideas to him here and there on some show concepts. Mostly he would chuckle and tell me to go back to the drawing board. I had now figured out that he wasn't such a scary guy after all, and in fact, there was tremendous favor over his and his wife's lives. God had used Tore in many ways to bring about His purposes for the medium of television. He had extraordinary wisdom about it all and was very knowledgeable about the industry. He also had incredible contacts and I knew it would be best to hang out near the goal post, so to speak.

One day Tore asked me to prepare and send him a demo reel for a new program. I didn't even ask for which organization it might be. I trusted Tore and if he asked for something like that, there was probably a good reason. I also knew opportunities would come and go, so I couldn't get my hopes up too high. I just had to trust God that He would orchestrate all things to work together for good.

A few weeks had passed when Tore said, in his nonchalant way, that things were progressing and he might need me to fly out to Ontario to meet the executives for a new show. Finally I asked what organization was interested in the show. "The 700 Club," he said. *I almost fell over! Seriously, THE 700 Club? I loved Pat Robertson!*

Tore said the show would be completely Christian and I would be able to share about Jesus every day on the show. I just stared at the wall in disbelief. This was such an amazing fulfillment of what God had called me to do several years ago. I exhaled and breathed in.

I clearly remember looking at the wispy formation of clouds out the window as I flew to Hamilton, Ontario. *Was this really happening?* I began to pray—not just one of those casual prayers. This was an earnest and serious prayer. I was in awe, once again, of life's incredible path.

*Dear God, I'm shocked at this journey. I totally understand if You think I am the wrong person for this important work. I wish I had done everything right in my life. I wish I could be a more spotless vessel, but I know it isn't about me anyway, and I just remembered I am spotless because of what You did for me at Calvary. You have clothed me in Your righteousness and have adorned me with jewels. I am beautified and dignified as royalty, adopted into Your family.*

*Father, I don't know if my journey can be useful, but I will spend the rest of my life telling people what Jesus did to take our pain and shame. If You can use my past to let people know that You love the broken, the shattered and the disqualified and that You never give up on us, You have all of me!*

I wiped a tear and hoped no one could hear me sniffling. In the book of Ruth, I love the posture and position Ruth took as she found herself widowed and in a new land with her mother-in-law. She knew that she needed someone to love and embrace her. She was a Moabite. Moabites did not have a good reputation because their people had been derived from an incestuous relationship.

In Ruth 2:2, Ruth said to Naomi, "Let me go to the fields and pick up the leftover grain behind anyone in whose eyes I find favor" (NIV). Ruth was willing to take the leftovers; she didn't feel she deserved special treatment. You probably know the story of how Boaz saw Ruth and instructed his workers to let some handfuls of grain fall on purpose for her to glean and not to rebuke her.

Then Ruth humbled herself profusely as she lay down at the feet of Boaz, making herself vulnerable to his rejection. God resists the proud, but gives grace to the poor in spirit. Her attitude invoked the favor of God over her life. Boaz was a sign and type of Christ Jesus redeeming us, His lost and disreputable children. "Boaz said to her, I have been made fully aware of all you have done for your mother-in-law since the death of your husband, and how you have left your father and mother and the land of your birth and have come to a people unknown to you before. The Lord recompense you for what you have done, and a full reward be given you by the Lord, the God of Israel, under Whose wings you have come to take refuge!" (Ruth 2:11-12).

Boaz did not reject Ruth for her heritage, but rather acknowledged what she had done by faith. He married her and she became engrafted into the direct lineage of Jesus. An incredible destiny was given to a woman no one knew—who gave up everything to become part of a new land and a different people.

I met the amazing folks at The 700 Club Canada. What a beautiful group of people. I shared my heart and connected with the lovely Gayle Brown, who served as Vice President of Finance and Administration. She had a heart of gold and I quickly fell in love with both her and her husband. They were true servants of the Lord and gave their lives to minister to Canadian people.

The months that followed were too fun for words to describe. We did several pilots with different male hosts. I kept wondering if I would have to go up against another potential female host for the show, but none ever showed up. It was as if this job was meant for me. I prayed grateful prayers under my breath. The first time I spoke with Brian Warren, I knew he was the right person with whom to co-host. His powerful voice and the anointing when he prayed were palpable. I loved him right away, even though he was certainly opposite of my flamboyant personality.

I thought it was humorous that God kept putting me with African American men, or in this case African-Canadian, to do TV shows. Of course, I loved to repeat my joke that I was more African than them because I was actually born in Africa! Brian was chosen as my partner for the new show so we flew down to meet Pat Robertson's executive to pass the final test of approval. That was a little nerve-racking to say the least. *What if they didn't like me? What if they felt I wasn't good enough?* I laid my worries to rest and trusted God to work out the details.

First I met John Turver and was immediately at ease with his deep love for God and his appreciation for the work of The 700 Club. He had the kindest and most sincere way about him. You could feel the profound relationship with God that emanated from his spirit. I immediately thought the world of him.

Both Brian and I were scheduled to meet with Pat's right hand man, Michael Little, of whom I had heard that "you don't want to mess with him." I was the first to be escorted to his office by his assistant. It was a long and daunting walk down that hallway. My heart beat rapidly as destiny seemed to hang in the balance of this next meeting.

All of my anxiety was laid to rest within the first couple minutes of our meeting. I liked him very much and he made me feel welcome. I think our meeting went well. We ended up talking much longer than expected, so his assistant came to let him know it was time for the daily devotions downstairs. I followed Mr. Little into a beautiful room where worship and praise had already begun. I could sense the Holy Spirit and thought how amazing it would be to work for an organization that put such emphasis on prayer in the middle of the day.

After devotions, we headed to lunch. Tore was also seated at our table. I glanced over to see if his face betrayed any unhappiness, but I could not see any signs. There was a lot of man talk at the table about sports and things of masculine importance. I enjoyed my soup and welcomed the opportunity to hear all of them speak so fervently together.

Gordon Robertson dropped by our table to say hello and told us a little about the Christian Broadcast Network's journey. His passion was evident and his work with *Superbook*, an incredible state-of-the-art animation series that brings the timeless stories of the Bible to life, was outstanding. Children's lives across the world have been significantly impacted by this initiative. What struck me most about Gordon was his easy going style and the kindness in his eyes. I thoroughly enjoyed hearing him share the vision he had to see the world won for Christ.

I was the only woman sitting at the table so I found myself rather tongue-tied in the shadow of these profound men of influence. I silently took note of the spacious place God had brought all of us to, who are wholly devoted to Him. There was a magnificent evidence of grace that rested over the entire CBN foundation and I pondered how honored I would be to serve them.

A few weeks later, we met with the Canadian arm of the CBN ministry, the Christian Broadcasting Associates' (CBA) board in Hamilton, Ontario. I was honored to be prayed over by them along with the beautiful co-host of The 700 Club, Miss America 1973, Terry Meeuwsen; the Vice President of Finance and Administration, Gayle Brown, whom I had grown to deeply respect; and Pat Robertson's long-time assistant, Barbara Johnson, who had always said that working for Pat was like trying to lay tracks in front of a speeding locomotive. I felt the power of God in that boardroom as I accepted the mantle and the blessing from the Lord through their sanction. I felt like the woman described in Proverbs 31:25 who is clothed with strength and dignity, who can laugh at the days to come.

There are some experiences in life that you can only laugh at later. The tragic yet brilliantly crafted test from the Lord in the following account is one of those stories. I am just now able to get a slight chuckle, while those who hear this account seem to find my pain quite hilarious! I thought I had learned all I needed to learn about where my identity lay. God had broken me beyond belief, what more could there be?

Tore called and said that the 50th year celebration of the Christian Broadcast Network would be taking place in Virginia Beach on October 1, 2011. Due to Pat Robertson's very busy schedule, we would have only one opportunity to have an on-camera interview with him for our Canadian show. Brian Warren would be unable to do the interview due to a prior commitment, but would meet us later for the event and Tore asked me if I was willing to fly down to do the interview alone.

*Are you kidding me?* I was over the moon. The incredible walk of faith that Pat Robertson had journeyed for the last 50 years had been phenomenal. Starting a station on just nickels in the bank and believing God for everything he needed made Pat Robertson my hero. His destiny has impacted the world, with healings, words of knowledge and the impartation of the power of the Holy Spirit he found in his living room many years ago. I stand amazed at the call of God on his life to the media and the power that television has to bring the gospel to all nations.

Today, CBN is one of the largest television ministries on the globe, reaching 200 countries with the powerful message of the gospel every single day. The 700 Club began to broadcast in 1966 and has an average daily audience of over one million viewers across the U.S. Fifty years and two days later, the Canadian version of the show was launching and it was the most incredible honor I had ever received to be a part of it.

So off I went to meet Pat Robertson and as I arrived at the Chicago O'Hare airport, I was amazed to find the gate to my connecting flight to Norfolk, Virginia, was less than a minutes' walk away. There it was, Gate C5, clear as day! *Awesome,* I whispered under my breath as I grabbed a coffee at the kiosk and noted on the large listing of arrivals and departures that my flight was delayed.

Well that was just fine with me, because I had lots of writing to do for the upcoming shoot for The 700 Club Canada in about four days. I became engrossed in my writing for the next hour and a half. Finally, I gathered my stuff and went to look at the board again. Still it said my flight was delayed.

I went and sat back down where I could clearly see the desk at Gate C5 and noted that no one was there yet. All seemed quiet and I had travelled enough now to know there are always delays with flights; there's nothing you can do but enjoy the wait. I was in the center of the long wing of the airport. There were probably 150 or so people sitting in the vicinity. On a whim, I leaned towards the blonde gentleman two seats down and asked him if he was waiting for the flight to Norfolk. He informed me he was and I naturally thought that most people in this area would be waiting for the same plane; after all, we were all sitting right in front of Gate C5.

He then gave my heart great comfort by informing me he was monitoring the status of our flight with his Blackberry. The flight was still delayed and I asked if he would let me know if anything changed. I went back to my inspired writing and at least 45 minutes passed. Finally, I really needed to go to the bathroom. I told him I would be back and I noted he did have a somewhat perplexed look on his face, as he seemed to be scrolling through information on his Blackberry. He smiled and nodded at me.

I looked over to the desk at Gate C5 and still, no one was there. I had not heard one single announcement about the flight. *When will we get going? This is starting to get a little tiring!*

As I straightened my hair in the bathroom, a woman emerged from a stall and asked me if the cell phone she just found was mine. It wasn't, so I tried to help her rummage through the contacts to see if we could figure out how to get it back to the owner. Finally, she simply said she would hand it in at customer service.

I had been in the bathroom about eight or nine minutes. I quickly headed back out to wait for the endlessly delayed flight. As I got back to the seats, I could not see the blonde fellow anywhere. Perhaps he had gone to the washroom. The desk at Gate C5 was still empty.

Before I sat back down, I thought I should check the board again to see if there had been any updates on the status of my flight. I casually walked over and looked high above my head. As I scanned the departures I found my flight number and let my eyes go to the far right where it said "Closed." *CLOSED?!!!! How can it be closed when it's been delayed for hours and I haven't heard one call to board the flight? That is not possible, just not possible!!*

I walked directly over to the desk at C5. Nothing made sense. I looked down the long row of windows and could see there was a plane outside of the next gate over. Bolting down there, I found a clearly visible identical sign that also said C5. I started taking short breaths and adrenalin began pumping through my body. There was no one at this desk either. I walked up to the door for the long walkway to the plane and I could see an employee way down at the end. I leaned over and looked out the window and something screamed inside of me, *That's your plane*!!

I banged on the door with my hand. The people sitting in the chairs right beside the door asked me if I was going to Norfolk. When I answered that yes, I was, a woman told me they had just closed the gate. I gasped, "That can't be! That's my plane, I didn't hear any announcements." I felt queasy. "Did you see a blonde guy go through?" Yes, they all nodded! "He just ran on at the last minute," a healthy larger woman calmly stated as she clasped her hands over her purse up against her stomach. I couldn't breathe and my legs felt weak.

I started banging louder on the door, startling an elderly woman sitting nearby. I had become one of those crazed people you see on that reality airport series! The employee still standing at the end of the causeway could not hear me. I yelled "HEY!" as if that would help. I was startled suddenly by a very cross looking woman behind me who asked, "Ma'am what is the problem?" Thank God, an employee that could actually hear me!

I explained that my plane was sitting right there and I had to be on it! I could not possibly miss this flight; my life hung in the balance, I told her as I shook my head with my most serious look. I begged her to please get me on that aircraft. "I'm sorry. This flight is closed and there is no way to let you on."

"No, that cannot be. You don't understand, I have been here for hours waiting at C5, ...the other C5 down there somewhere," I pointed towards the fake C5, "and I have not been paged or called..."

She didn't make eye contact as she shuffled her important papers on the desk. "We are under no obligation to call your name ma'am!" she replied. I told her that I had a paid ticket for this flight and the plane was right there! "There is nothing I can do, the flight is closed!" she replied.

I felt dizzy and hung onto the desk for comfort. I inhaled. *Is there carbon monoxide poisoning in the air?* I looked to my right at Gate C6 and there was a more official looking woman standing there with a necktie on. I hurried over to talk to her and grasping her sleeve I said, "My plane is sitting there and I was at the wrong C5 and a lady lost her cell phone in the bathroom, can you get me on?"

"What?" the manager looked perplexed.

"Please, I have to be on that flight. You have no idea how important this is to my life. Please can you do something?"

Perhaps she took pity on me or maybe she feared I might become a security risk. She pressed her lips together and walked towards C5. I could only assume she intended to rectify this disastrous mistake.

There was a young Rastafarian looking guy manning Gate C6, maybe he could help me. "No ma'am, when a gate is closed, it is closed. You cannot get on that flight." I asked how long it would take me to drive to Norfolk. He lifted one edge of his mouth and spoke out the side of his face and said, "Ma'am, that would take you about 12 hours. That's not really an option."

Of course it was an option! "I'm a good driver!" I informed him.

Where did that lady manager go? I swung around and headed back to C5. My heels clacked loudly on the floor. *God would definitely not let me miss the most important trip of my life to interview Pat Robertson. For Pete's sake, this cannot be happening!* "God's got my back, hemmed in before and behind, I'm the head and not the tail and I'm calling those things that are not, as though they are." I noticed I was talking to myself.

At C5 I found the manager. "No, the plane is full, there is not one seat available. I have surveyed it myself. Your ticket has been sold to a bystander."

"Could you ask them to get off?" I enquired, blinking rapidly.

The manager shook her head and walked away. I could not feel my outer limbs and leaned my entire body against the high top desk, dropping my purse to the ground beside me. I felt my lungs caving in and my throat access restricting. *Are there firebugs flying around? I see white lights.* A cold sweat now pulsed through my upper torso and I looked around for some sort of sick bag. Taking my jacket off, I had lost the words to further complain or ask for any help.

I saw a look of pity come over the attendant's face for the first time, as I laid my forehead on the desk. I heard her clicking very fast on her keyboard and then she handed me a ticket and explained that I was booked on the earliest flight to Norfolk in the morning, which would arrive there at 9:37 a.m. I said thank you in a barely audible voice.

I began heading down the inner corridor of this cursed wing of the Chicago O'Hare airport. I had so many questions. *Isn't there some sort of FAA or TSA (whatever that stands for) regulation that they have to offload my baggage? I have no Replenishment Moisture Deep Activating Enrichment Jojoba Oil Conditioner Serum for my hair; it's in my suitcase.* As I passed the seats I had been comfortably resting in, I looked over at the fake Gate C5, and had to wonder what airport engineer came up with such a thing. Furthermore, how was it that I ended up sitting beside the one other blonde guy in the entire airport who was also at the wrong gate?

I needed to call and explain this to Tore. There was no way for me to logically clarify how this just happened. I tried to explain and he listened, but the words were not sufficient to express the sheer magnitude of apparently completely unrelated coincidences, which had contributed to this calamity that was too large to talk about at that moment.

"I messed up," I said as I sauntered down the endless promenade, looking like a lost toddler with a briefcase.

"I will let John know," he said. I wanted to cry, but people were already staring at me.

As I strolled down 2.3 miles of airport hallway, which was strangely and eerily empty, I found myself confronting my worst fear. *Idiocy.* I had missed an important flight…by sitting there waiting!! *How inept was I? Why did this happen?* I did not know how I would ever get over it. In a maze of long corridors that I am not even sure how I navigated alone, I came face to face with the basest level of my insecurity. It felt like I had just jeopardized everything God had done for the last ten years to get me here. It's interesting that in the heat of a crisis, life can look so bad and yet it is a completely irrational perspective.

Once on the shuttle, I looked at my reflection and realized that my hair looked exactly like dried out twigs in the fall because of an accidental hair over processing at the salon two days earlier. It looked like the prongs of a thousand misshapen forks. I prayed that I was at least on the right shuttle. The driver had informed me that there were two hotels with the same name. Obviously, the same guy who made two C5 gates thought they should also name a bunch of hotels the same name too.

By some sort of unexpected miracle, I arrived at the right hotel. I was offered the stress package toiletry kit, which apparently did not include scissors to trim my hair. I asked the clerk if I could borrow her scissors and I would return them shortly. She told me that I couldn't take them to my room for "security reasons." *Did this rule apply to everyone,* I wondered, *or just people who looked unstable?* She then paused and asked me what I needed them for. I pointed to my hair; with a knowing look, she handed them right to me. She told me strictly that I had to use them in the public washroom in the foyer and then return them. I agreed to her heavy-handed terms.

Going up the elevator was an exercise in restraint to keep from dropping to the fetal position. I couldn't take any more! My errors had cost people time and money. I didn't know how God could ever use me, dumb as I was. I got in the door of my hotel room and fell to the floor sobbing. I called JT. He had never heard me like this. He prayed for me immediately and I just hiccupped and sniffled loudly. I was inconsolable. "Can you find my suitcase with my hair moisture replenishment, rejuvenator, Jojoba activator serum, JT?" I had my priorities. Within minutes, he found out my suitcase was waiting for me at the baggage claim office in Norfolk. My plane had already landed at the destination by the time I actually got to my hotel. Would the misery never end?

I climbed into bed after texting a desperate message to my dear friend Sandi, who is always a prayer warrior on my behalf. I cried and prayed. *I'm so sorry God. I've let You down. Are You mad at me? I don't know how to fix this.* I felt a tiny, gentle whisper of peace flood over my being. I only knew one thing to do. God inhabits our praise. He literally comes down and dwells with those who will worship Him, especially in the very worst of times.

I began to declare what I knew to be true. *You are a faithful God. You know the end from the beginning. You will not abandon me in my time of need. You love me. I can trust You. I don't understand why this happened, but I know You are in control. Your love for me is unconditional. Nothing can separate me from You. Help me Jesus. Please God, give me strength to overcome this devastating night. I need You. You are all I have and it is enough. I love You, Jesus. I love You.* I fell asleep in prayer with a peace that passed all understanding carrying my mournful soul. I could not explain this terrible night, but I knew my Relentless Redeemer and He would be found true to me, even if my circumstances had conspired against me.

In the midst of this misfortune, I felt like I passed some kind of test. With all of the baggage that I personally had to release to God, I had become a new creation. I was grateful that my heart was steadfast in the end towards my Redeemer, when faced with a personally debilitating experience. I realize that it may be hard to comprehend what the breaking point is in another person's life, but for me, this trial stretched me to the core. Once again in my life I was confronted with the fear of loss, disappointment and failure.

John Turver was patiently waiting for me as I disembarked from the plane the next morning. He asked what happened and knew I was beyond disappointed. I expressed my deep sorrow and just shook my head with sadness. It was difficult to explain how this transpired. John was very sorry but explained that they would not mess with Pat's schedule in any way, so the interview had been completely cancelled. There would be no other opportunity to interview Mr. Robertson.

John had a lot of work to get done for the celebrations that would be taking place, so he dropped me off at the Founder's Inn in Virginia Beach and said we would have lunch later that day at the restaurant. I did the only thing that will make a desperate girl feel happy again - I got a pedicure and then went to the restaurant to meet John who had a warm smile on his face.

"I have some good news for you," he quipped. I stopped cold in my tracks and stared at him while I held my breath. I was hoping he didn't mean that they were serving rack of lamb on the menu. He explained he had spoken with Pat personally and told of my disappointment about the airport connection. Pat called his assistant to see if they could squeeze in a time to make this interview happen. *They'd found one slot, the following afternoon!*

In one of the most embarrassing public scenes I have ever made, I grabbed John's hand with both my hands and fell to my knees on the floor looking up at him. John casually looked around the restaurant and lifted me to my feet. It was a miracle how the intense pain in my chest that I had carried for 18 hours was suddenly gone. I had never felt such instantaneous relief of emotional agony in all my life.

The next day, Tore and Brian Warren arrived. The moment Pat walked on the set, I felt my eyes water with relief. It had all worked out; I didn't need to be so incredibly upset. Pat was a wonderful person with a magnificent spirit and we felt a prolific presence of God as we spoke on camera and he prayed a blessing over Canada and us.

My identity did not change with my circumstances. I remained a daughter of the Living God, dressed in royal robes - albeit whimpering alone through the airport with my crown of righteousness tipping sideways on my head. In this crisis and throughout the epic tale of my life, my security and heritage remained untouched. I received an incredible reminder once again that I was weak and would need my Relentless Redeemer to survive every hour, every day, and every new season for the rest of my days on earth.

# 14

# RELENTLESS REDEMPTION

*Even if you have been banished to the most distant land under the heavens, from there the Lord your God will gather you and bring you back.*

- Deuteronomy 30:4 NIV

I remember an incredible experience I had with my family on the Masai Mara in Kenya, East Africa. I spent the day photographing lions, elephants, cheetahs, baboons, zebras, ostriches, a black rhino with its baby, giraffes, wild boars, wart hogs, wildebeests, hippos, crocodiles, elands, gazelles and the most amazing birds I had ever seen. We were so close to a male lion that I shuddered to think what might happen if he decided he didn't like us. At one point in the day, our driver Joe, had to back up our safari vehicle real fast as a wild boar set his sights on ramming us. The day before, the elephants were so close, you could almost reach out and touch them. *What a staggering world!*

As we stood in our safari rover and stared in amazement at the vultures circling a dead carcass, my wonderful son, Aaron and beautiful daughter, Larissa were ecstatic to point out the next wild animal that caught their eye. My brother Jeff, his wife Elaine, and their three kids Rachel, Kaitlin and Ryan rode in the next safari car over waving, laughing and taking pictures.

I recall a strange feeling that came over me as the wind blew past my ears and messed up my hair as we crossed the plains. I felt completely alone. Obviously I wasn't alone, but in the middle of this vast grassland, I had a greater understanding of how small and insignificant I was. Breathing in the clean African air while surrounded by my favorite people in the whole world, I was still just one girl that no one could save but God.

We are born alone and ultimately we die alone. In between, we rub shoulders with friends, rub noses with lovers and rub sunscreen on our children. Yet, I have found that feeling of being alone never leaves me. It creeps over me when I have a huge deadline, like when I'm writing a book that no one can write for me. I feel alone when an attack of insecurity or an accusation from the accuser of the brethren attempts to remind me where I came from.

It's the moment you get a big award and then notice that no one else is as excited about it as you are. It's the day you finally get your dream job and the family just wants to know "what's for dinner?" In fact, our quest for true connection often leaves us hollow and our search for a soul mate frequently turns up empty in the end. Who knows why a passing comment pierces a wound we've tried to hide? Who knows what makes us laugh out loud? Although we bear one another's burdens to the best of our ability and gain consolation from a shoulder to lean on and a hand to hold, in truth, no one fully knows us...except our Relentless Redeemer.

In my younger years, the uncertainty of my "aloneness" caused me to be afraid. In my later years, I have learned something about myself: I am strong enough to feel alone and not fear it any longer, because it's quite simply not true. It's just a feeling. I could lose everything I have tomorrow: my family, my money, my career, my looks, my health, everything. But the one thing I won't lose is my God. He paid a price so monumental for my redemption that my value is now equivalent with the worth of the Sacrifice—priceless.

It is in God's understanding of your need that He made a promise, an incredible provision for that desperate longing in your soul. He has provided a Comforter who stands ready to embrace, support, defend and guide you. God knew that our human experience would crave relationship, yet not find that purest of love in the eyes of mankind so He bequeathed a gift to fill the void—providential provision accessed only through true intimacy with the Creator.

He is our life raft; a preserver that will carry us during the blackest of nights, the stormiest of seasons and the most desperate of days. He gives us an unwavering guarantee of understanding, tenderness and affection, regardless of our performance. It is only in receiving and accepting this extraordinary companionship that we will find a Friend who stays closer than a brother.

He is the lover, the enduring provider and the sustainer of you. He is the whisper in the wind as you walk along the ocean and the encompassing blanket of peace that passes all understanding in the face of unspeakable tragedy. He is the power felt when weakness threatens to overwhelm. He is the strength you need to press towards the mark, the confidante who guards your reputation and the One who walks through the garden right beside you when others have ventured down their own destiny's path. The purest of truth reveals that through it all, you are never, *never* alone.

We are given repeated assurances of this truth throughout the Word of God, as seen in Deuteronomy 31:8, "It is the Lord Who goes before you; He will [march] with you; He will not fail you or let you go or forsake you; ...fear not, neither become broken [in spirit— depressed, dismayed, and unnerved with alarm]."

Now I thank the Lord for this journey—for every devastating decision and sorrowful moment, for the mountaintops and valleys - I give Him praise. Without the failures that I had experienced, I would not have the wisdom to bear the providence of the place I am today. Without God grinding me to dust and remaking me, I would not have the character or strength to sustain the call.

Today at church my pastor, Mike Poulin, spoke on how one small seed will produce a crop that has infinite possibilities. I only had one seed left - Christ's gift of redemption. It was all I had. As I allowed the seed of redemption to take root in the foundation of my soul, I discovered, to the glory of God alone, it has yielded a relentless harvest and is unstoppable by any man.

My former pastor, Bob Peragallo, who walked with me during the worst storm of my life, recently sent me this unsolicited note.

*Laura-Lynn, you've come a long way with your life and ministry.*
*It still amazes me how wonderful this God that we worship is. I*

*remember back when I first arrived and you were leading worship for us. You would always talk about what your week was like (in between songs). I remember one Sunday morning saying to myself, "This girl has no message." Twenty-some years later and a lot of hard life and persistence in seeking God, you've got the message and the platform to speak it. I am very proud of you as a person and friend. Keep up the good work, God has a big investment in you and this message is worth it all. As Leo Durocher once said, "Baseball is like church. Many attend but few understand."*

As time and Jesus heal, an incredible, collective awe transpires. Years later, we marvel at His unyielding work. We laugh out loud at what God does when friends pray, hearts repent and God forgives. Don't give up when the bitter cold of winter threatens your hope and future. Don't quit when your own heart of iniquity has brought about a justifiable demise and all seems lost. It's not over. There stands a Father who will not give up on pursuing His wayward prodigal child. The seeds that will bring forth your destiny and greatest purpose must die in the cold, desolate ground, before they can give birth to the beautiful creation you were born to be.

I am grateful for the grace of God, which never let me go and did not disqualify me in my errors. Through the profundity of the precious blood of Jesus, I am able to stand in His righteousness and boldly declare to the world that Jesus is the answer for the lost, broken and hurting. He has been my answer in the darkness, and now I speak with authority and personal knowledge that Jesus loves us—this I know. His unconditional, outrageous favor is ours for the asking in faith with humility, knowing it is He who does every great work and it will never be our own doing.

I have shared this as a testimony to those who battle rejection, failure, pain and shame. I pray my life reflects what God can truly do with those who think they have irreparably lost their way and gives hope to those who may be tempted to give up on the broken, straggling ones around them. Failure is an event, not a person, as Zig Ziglar once said.

Looking back, the worst days have produced the best days. The pain has given way to peace. Brokenness has led to wholeness and the One who bore it in my place has redeemed my shame. I remain staggered at life's turn of events. He loved me in my weakness, never left my side through failure, and brought me out the other side to victory. God knows our frame—that we are weak and in need of a powerful Savior. He never meant for us to be perfect; He is. His love covers a multitude of sins.

To every decimated life, He brings joy. To the sick, He brings healing. To the shattered, He brings hope. The disqualified, He qualifies. For the weak, He becomes your strength. All that the enemy has stolen will be returned and restored. As Joel 2:25 says, "So I will restore to you the years that the swarming locust has eaten, the crawling locust, the consuming locust, and the chewing locust" (NKJV).

Days full of hope that stagger and confound the mind lay just beyond the most brutal of seasons. It is by crossing the wilderness that a promised land is found. God will never leave you in the place your own works have brought you. His power is inconceivable and His love unstoppable. He ceaselessly calls your name and He will never let you go. He is today, and will always be *your Relentless Redemption.*